Coaching a Spread No-Huddle Offense

Craig Johnston

COACHES CHOICE™

ISBN: 978-1-60679-348-0
Library of Congress Control Number: 2015959985
Book layout: Cheery Sugabo
Cover design: Cheery Sugabo

Coaches Choice
P.O. Box 1828
Monterey, CA 93942
www.coacheschoice.com

Coach Craig Johnston's spread offensive attack has been causing defensive coordinators nightmares for years. Like any great offensive scheme, his system is built on sound fundamentals, and this book tells coaches how to implement the spread from the ground up.

Buck Roggeman
Former Head Football Coach
Pacific Grove (CA) High School

Craig Johnston has proven over the years that he is an innovator and a great football mind who understands where the game has come from and where it is going. This book is a great read for any high school football coach looking to run a high-powered program as well as a fun and explosive offensive system.

Pat Johnston
Head Football Coach
San Luis Obispo (CA) High School

Coach Johnston has conceived a system that adapts to any level of play. His comprehensive book will provide the inexperienced as well as the experienced coach with a strong foundation as they move forward in their coaching career. His ideas and concepts are battle tested and successful. This book is a must for any coach looking to develop a successful, explosive offensive system.

Dean Herrington
Head Football Coach
Bishop Alemany High School (CA)

Dedication

This book is dedicated to my wife Patty "Cakes" and my three sons Pat, Phil, and Ken.

Cakes is the most supportive wife and team "Mom" a coach could ask for. The Johnston boys accounted for over 15,000 yards of offense during their high school careers and were an absolute joy to coach.

To Mom, Dad, Janel, Pam, and Jill.

To my high school football coach at St. Paul High School, 1976, Marijon Ancich. 360 high school wins. Mentor to nearly 60 high school head football coaches. His approach and knowledge of the game of football as well as his wife Jacquie making me a part of their family have made a lasting impact on me.

Acknowledgments

Thanks to the many coaches that spent their valuable time helping me be a better coach. Thank you for giving me an opportunity to learn from you throughout the years. I consider myself a student of the game of football, and I am thankful that you were my teachers. Bill Walsh, Tom Craft, Mouse Davis, Terry Shea, Ted Tollner, Mike White, Jeff Tedford, Don Coryell, Monte Clark, Steve Clarkson, and more.

Special thanks to my high school coach Marijon Ancich, St. Paul High School, 1976. I would not be writing this book if it were not for him. Coach Ancich retired last year as the second-winningest high school football coach in California history. His coaching pedigree has produced nearly 60 high school head football coaches. My love and passion for football come from him. His knowledge of the game, ability to motivate players and coaches, and insight into the many details of offensive and defensive football have been invaluable to me.

Thanks to Coach Bill Walsh, with whom I worked at his quarterback camps at Stanford. Thanks, Coach, for spending one-on-one time with me watching film. I heard what you said, and it works!

Thank you Coach Joe Harper, My Head Coach at Cal Poly San Luis Obispo, 1980. The leader of our 1980 Division II National Championship. Quiet but strong. Perfect illustration of "lead by example."

Thank you Coach Dave Grosz, my quarterback coach at Cal Poly, San Luis Obispo, 1980. Coach Grosz taught me how to be a championship quarterback.

Thank you Coach John Crivello, my quarterback/wide receiver coach at Cal Poly, San Luis Obispo, 1980. His mastery and enthusiasm for the passing game have been my cornerstones.

I am very grateful to Tom Craft, former head coach at Palomar Junior College, Mt. Sac Junior College, and current head football coach at Riverside Community College. Former head coach and offensive coordinator at San Diego State, Tom has coached numerous state and national championship teams. His vast knowledge of the spread no-huddle offense and his willingness to share have been a tremendous help. Tom's grasp of the subtleties and nuances of an up-tempo, explosive, and versatile no-huddle attack have had a tremendous influence on me and my philosophy.

I am very grateful to Dean Herrington, currently the head football coach at Alemany High School. Dean is one of the elite coaches in the highly competitive CIF Southern Section of California. His knowledge of the spread no-huddle offense and how to run it are second to none. His willingness to spend long hours, sharing his ideas and philosophies with me is very much appreciated.

Thank you to Coach Monte Clark, head coach of the Detroit Lions and San Francisco 49ers and offensive line coach of the 1972 Miami Dolphins, who taught me that no passing game will work if you don't protect the quarterback. His tips on pass protections, technique, head/feet priority, and running game schemes have been extremely helpful. (Sorry for the exploding golf ball, Coach!)

Thanks to Joe Englebrecht and Pat Ryan, my junior high football coaches at St. Brunos, Whittier. These men taught me throwing mechanics, play concepts, and how to compete. I was lucky to learn many of the concepts in this book at an early age.

Thanks to my coaching staff at Carmel High School. Golden Anderson, Bill Swift, Devin Meheen, and Mike Herro. Special thanks to Coach Anderson for allowing me to stay involved. His additions, subtractions, and tweaking of our SNH offense has it evolving and firing on all cylinders. You are all great coaches and a lot of fun to work with.

Thanks to Buck Roggeman, former head coach at Pacific Grove High School. Buck made me a better coach by producing well-coached, spirited teams I had to compete against every year. His enthusiasm as well as technical knowledge of offense and defense always had his teams motivated and prepared. His help and advice on this book is much appreciated.

Thanks to Erik Halbrend and Ralph Ward for their technical advice, Debbie French for her photographs, and John Blankfort for the cover picture.

Contents

Preface

"I want the big play. I'm not going to stay up all night trying to figure out how to gain three yards."

—Sid Gilman

Hi, Coach! If you're like me, you are probably in the lobby of a nice hotel during a break from a clinic or convention and decided to take a look at the hundreds of instructional books and DVDs for sale. Like me, you want to become a better coach. You're reading this because you are a coach that runs a spread no-huddle (SNH) offense, or a coach that runs an offensive system other than the spread that wants to spice it up. You want to know the best way to learn an exciting new system. If this is the case, then keep reading.

"What am I doing?"

About 25 years ago, it hit me during a late-night film session. I was tired of diagramming every run-blocking pattern against every defense, executing it at game time, and gaining minimal yardage. It was frustrating having all those defenders in the box. I was meticulous in attempting to make sure every defensive guy was blocked against every conceivable defense. All that work to gain two yards! We always had a hat on a hat, but the offense was stagnant. What am I doing? Everybody's blocked, but we're going nowhere! I took a good look at what I was trying to do with the players I had. I decided that there had to be a better way of producing more points per minute of prep time. I needed to get out of my comfort zone and do what was best for the type of athletes we had. I decided to implement the SNH offense and was determined to research every bit of information from the best sources, making sure I learned as much as I could from great coaches that had run the SNH successfully. I made myself a pest, and it paid off!

Did My Homework

Tons of SNH books and videos are available out there. I've read and/or watched most of them: the spread, the spread no-huddle, the hurry-up no-huddle, the hurry-up spread no-huddle, the slow-down spread no-huddle, the fly no-huddle, and so on. It's mind-boggling the amount of information out there. I've learned a lot. Persistence and curiosity has enabled me the luck to pick the brains of some of the most knowledgeable coaches that have ever worn a whistle. Great coaches who were willing to spend their valuable time helping a student of the game, like me. I asked questions, shut up, listened, and then implemented. Most of the ideas in this book did not come from me. Most are borrowed. Borrowed from supremely competent, battle tested coaches who generously loaned me, gave me, bits and pieces of their vast expertise. This book shows you what the puzzle looks like when you put all the pieces together.

Over the last 25 years, our team has had a quarterback that threw for over 8,000 yards and 93 career touchdowns as well as numerous quarterbacks who have thrown for over 2,000 yards in a season and 5,000 yards for a career. We've had many wide receivers with well over 1,000 yards receiving per season as well as running backs that have rushed for over 2,000. Most importantly, we are scoring points!

This book is broken into chapters with many sub-headings for an easier read. Glance through it, and you will see tried-and-proven ways to implement or supercharge an SNH offense, or any offense for that matter. Thousands of hours of research and over 30 years of trial and error in one easy-to-read guide. Enjoy!

Introduction

My "Magic" Moment

"Success: it is what you get outta what you got."

—Woody Hayes

My "magic" moment occurred to me while watching, on a 16 mm projector, Mouse Davis's Portland State team go up and down the field on an opponent, scoring 100 points. I was a player at Cal Poly San Luis Obispo watching scout film. We were to play them the following week. It was freakish looking. Wide receivers all over the place, motioning back and forth to determine pre-snap coverage. Each offensive lineman in a two-point stance every play, with at least one of his feet a yard in the backfield, sitting on his heels in preparation to pass block. While under center, quarterback Neil Lomax was practically facing backward with one foot already into the first step of his drop. He and every one of his teammates didn't give a darn that they were giving away pass. They were going to throw the ball every down no matter what. The ball was snapped with receivers going in all sorts of predetermined directions when they would stop, adjust, or keep going based on what the defense did. Wide receivers going in every direction would, out of nowhere, throw up a hand and either stop, go in, or go out. This was the true read-on-the-run run-and-shoot. It had all the answers. If you covered deep, they would throw up a hand and throw short and vice versa. If you covered the perimeter, they would throw inside. Wide receivers all over the place, throwing their hands up wide open! At least two guys were open on every play! Witnessing that convinced me there was another way to attack defenses.

No-Huddle Fits Any Offensive Attack

The spread no-huddle (SNH) concepts in this book can be applied to any offense. You can pre-align, signal, and execute your own offensive scheme using the no-huddle concepts in this book. You can supercharge any offensive scheme. If you take the spread out of spread no-huddle and plug in your particular attack, you will make it faster, more productive, and a lot more fun. Imagine doing everything you already do faster and more efficiently. Supercharge your existing offense by not huddling. Take an existing, potent offense and accelerate it. That is tough to defend.

SNH Offers Diversity

The SNH attack is diverse. Chances are it has something that will fit your talent pool. It offers a myriad of options for the coach who must determine a plan of attack based on the unique skill set of his team. With the SNH, there is no reason to feel like your offensive attack is doomed just because you lack dominating players. The SNH not only gives you balance between run and pass, but also balance between which players handle the ball.

The spread is obviously an excellent way of passing the football. When you get into the SNH, you gain tremendous advantages in the passing game by spreading people out, but it's that spreading out that allows you to be more successful running the ball. The vertical and horizontal stretch of the SNH opens up passing and running lanes you don't have with a typical 21 (two running backs, one tight end) offense. By not having to block as many guys in the box and having them as condensed as they are in a normal formation, running lanes are bigger and more abundant. By spreading the defense out, you force them to defend every player from sideline to sideline, opening up vertical running and passing lanes by mere formation. By not huddling you dictate tempo. This allows you to run more or fewer plays, score quicker, create defensive anxiety, make checks and audibles easier, and it's difficult to simulate in practice. When you combine the no-huddle tempos with an offense that appears complicated, but is simple to run, you become tough to defend.

What Is Balanced?

I call balanced 50-50 run to pass while equally distributing who touches the ball.

I've listened to coaches talk about having balance in their offensive attack. What does balanced actually mean? Balance between what? I am genuinely unsure of what they are talking about. The SNH facilitates a balance of many characters and play calls. Balance between run and pass, quarterback and tailback, X and Z, screen and dropback, give or pitch? What does a balanced offensive attack look like?

Coaches who don't run a spread no-huddle attack speak of the balance they have implemented into their offense. They describe running the ball 70 percent of the time now rather than 85 percent. I understand if they have a player who is so dominant, it doesn't matter that they are predictable. "Why be balanced if I don't have to be?" Point well taken. Whatever it takes to come out one point ahead of the other guy is the most important thing. If you have one guy who can carry or pass the ball 70 percent of the time and win, then do it! In my 30-plus years of coaching, I've had maybe a handful of players that fit that mold. Most of the time, I'm trying to be as creative as I can to utilize the talent on my team. If you coach long enough, you tell stories of the stud you once had. It's what you do the rest of the years that we are discussing. What are you doing offensively when you don't have a "horse" to jump on? What are you doing to squeeze out the most productivity with the players you have? I chose the SNH because it allows me to *amoeba-size* myself from year to year. (I just made up a new word: amoeba-size.) I can ride the "horse" if I have one, or matriculate the ball downfield without one.

An Assorted Offensive Menu

Many different offensive systems are available out there. Any system executed with precision will work. I choose the SNH system because it offers diversity. I don't have to be dominant at any one thing on a consistent basis. I've got options every year.

The combination of the spread offensive system and multi-tempo no-huddle pace is tough to stop. The SNH attack gives you choices based on your personnel. If you have a great offensive line, it doesn't matter. You can do anything you want.

Run Game

Option: Zone read, mid-line, triple, lead, speed, power.

Shovel: A great way to block option but show pass.

Power: Can be run a zillion ways with interchangeable personnel.

Zone read: Zone read principles can be applied to most run-actions.

Trap: A great way to combat defensive line aggressiveness while getting angles.

Counter: If you can't block them head on, block down.

Draw: Tailback draw, quarterback draw, wraparound draw, bubble draw, "Boise draw."

Reverse: Take advantage of undisciplined backside players. Sometimes they work!

Pass Game

Sprint: Aids quarterback vision. Helps quarterback run away from pressure in a controlled manner.

Dropback: Requires good footwork by quarterback and solid protection from offensive line.

Play-action: Most effective when married to potent run game. See *Sprint*.

Quick: The quick game in shotgun requires two steps deeper for wide receivers on initial stem.

Screen: Great versus blitz. Wide receiver, slot, tailback, tight end, and draw screens are all high-percentage passes.

Gadget plays: Big play potential. Exploit undisciplined or overaggressive defenders.

SNH Is Fun

The SNH is fun. You will get more people in the stands because the SNH is thrilling to watch. Fans like the big-gainers and the ball in the air. Players like the fact that they have an opportunity to show their talents. This entices the non-football skill-type players to your program. You'll get basketball, track, and baseball guys to come out for your team because they see that your style of play is exciting. These guys may not view themselves as football-type players. You must convince them otherwise. You would like them to view your SNH attack as a version of basketball on the football field. Giving them basketball-like things to do on the football field helps. Facilitate a smooth transition from one sport to the other by requiring skills that utilize similar musculature movement. Basketball players make great possession receivers, and track guys are deep threats. Tell your basketball, baseball, wrestling, track, and water polo athletes they will catch a bunch of passes, they will get their name in the newspaper, and girls like guys who get their name in the newspaper. If that doesn't work, then I can't help you.

"Look for players with character and ability. But remember, character comes first."

—Joe Gibbs

What to Look for in Your Quarterback

Quarterbacks come in all shapes, size, intellect, and maturity. Very few coaches are blessed with the 6'4" flame thrower or the nimble runner who runs 4.4 in the 40. Some are very smart, and some are not. Some are a dual threat, and some are zero threats. What you see is what you get, and it is your job to make him the best he can be. His make-up could be any combination of different mental, physical, and emotional characteristics. Maybe he is very good at a couple of things and mediocre at a bunch of things, or vice versa. Maybe his limitations are more mental and emotional. He is what he is. It is up to you to find out what he can do best and utilize his talents. Find what it is your quarterback *can* do, and coach to his strengths!

This chapter is broken into two parts:
- Physical traits
- Intangibles (mental and emotional aspects of quarterbacking)

I have tried to learn as much as I can from many great quarterback coaches. I have listened intently as they discuss the art of quarterbacking. I have also worked with some outstanding and not-so-outstanding quarterbacks at the Division I, Division II, junior college, and high school level. Most of us have never coached a quarterback that can do it all. Most quarterbacks are better at some things more than others. The players are different from year to year. They experience the same issues that young men have always faced, but they differ physically, mentally, and emotionally. Consider yourself lucky to discover a gem, but don't get frustrated when your quarterback doesn't have the looks or skills that you have had in the past. Feel good that you have a system that does not depend on your quarterback to be a superstar. The most important thing your quarterback must do is execute the game plan and get the team from point A to point B, with point B being the end zone.

Physical Quarterback Traits

The following are traits to look for in your quarterback. They are not listed in terms of importance, but rather as a set of skills and abilities that you should look for when evaluating what it is that your quarterback can do.

Arm Strength

Arm strength is overrated. A quarterback with good vision, good judgment, and an ability to anticipate can make up for a lack of arm strength. Arm strength is nice to have, but useless without common sense and good decision making. The problem sometimes associated with strong-armed quarterbacks is the tendency to throw into a crowd of defenders. They firmly believe that because they have a "rocket" arm, they can fit the ball into windows that are nonexistent or very small. Some, not all, strong-armed quarterbacks think they can wait a fraction of a second more to allow their receiver to open up before delivering the ball, rather than anticipating where the receiver will be and delivering the ball on time. This situation often results in a sack. Many strong-armed quarterbacks overestimate their ability to throw between defenders. They believe that they will deliver the ball with so much zip that it will get to the receiver before the defensive back can make a play. Many quarterbacks force the ball into a crowd because they believe their arm strength can overcome good defense.

It is not wise to generalize and label your quarterback one way or another, so be careful with the young strong-armed kid. Do not let the strength of his arm sway him from making the same reads and executing the timing necessary to the play. His pocket clock should be the same regardless of his arm strength.

Give Your Strong-Armed Quarterback Some Help

Having a strong-armed quarterback can be a real luxury. It is easier to teach a strong-armed quarterback how to release the ball faster, make better decisions, and develop touch than ask a weak-armed quarterback to be able to throw the ball deep or with more velocity. Your quarterback may be young, strong, and raw. It is your job to arm him with the other important traits he needs to become a fully functioning spread no-huddle (SNH) quarterback. With an ability to put touch on the ball and good decision making, a quarterback with a strong arm can be a great thing. He can probably throw the ball a long way, so threatening the defense by throwing the ball deep becomes a possibility. The vertical passing attack can be a real game-changer, and having a quarterback who can throw deep is a real blessing.

Be careful not to get too wrapped up in arm strength when evaluating your quarterback prospects. An average-armed quarterback with good vision and decision making is sometimes better than the strong-armed quarterback with no feel for the game.

Release

The release point of your quarterback is crucial. The best example of a great release point is Peyton Manning. He not only releases the ball at a very high point, but his pre-release (set) stance is such that he gets the ball from his set point to release extremely quickly. If you watch Manning drop back, notice where he places the ball during his dropback. The ball is set above his numbers, often above his shoulders near his right ear. Remember, the quicker the motion from the time the quarterback makes his decision to throw to the time he actually releases the ball, the less time the defense has to react. Having the ball set high prior to release facilitates a quick release.

As a coach, you walk a fine line sometimes when you mess with a quarterback's release, especially when coming out of baseball season. The baseball release is more of a windup, where the ball comes down before it comes up. This is not how a football is thrown. Defensive backs love quarterback's that wind up. They will break on a receiver when the quarterback begins his long baseball windup and have time to react and defend/intercept the pass. Whatever you can do to get your quarterback to release the ball quickly is key. Coach your quarterbacks to exaggerate setting the ball high above the shoulders the entire off-season (Figure 1-1) so when they put shoulder pads and helmet on, the ball settles at the top of the numbers, shoulder high (Figure 1-2). If the quarterback has used good ball positioning during the off-season, this should be a comfortable position once the helmet and shoulder pads come on.

Figure 1-1. Off-season ball set (no shoulder pads, helmet)

Figure 1-2. In-season ball set (shoulder pads, helmet)

The key points are as follows:

- A quick release is essential.
- High ball positioning facilitates a quick release.
- Off-season ball set. Exaggerate the ball high at all times (no shoulder pads, helmet).
- In-season ball set. No different than the off-season set, but shoulder pads and helmet bring the ball down "naturally." It is not a conscious adjustment for the quarterback.

The following sequence of pictures demonstrates how a high set (Figure 1-3) facilitates a high takeaway (Figure 1-4), which facilitates a high release (Figure 1-5). Notice the throwing thumb down during the follow-through to the opposite pocket (Figure 1-6). This release coupled with solid decision making can make a quarterback dangerous.

Figure 1-3. High set

Figure 1-4. High takeaway

Figure 1-5. High release

Figure 1-6. Follow-through

Touch

Certain situations in a game require the quarterback to reduce the velocity of the throw and make the ball more catchable for the receiver. These situations may require that the quarterback throw the ball over one defender and under another to drop the ball softly into his receiver's hands. The strong-armed quarterback with no touch will try to throw the ball *through* a defender rather than use touch. This results in interceptions and frustration for everyone involved. Touch involves taking a bit of velocity off to allow your receiver time to get to a ball. The majority of throws made in a game require some kind of touch. It is a rare occasion for a quarterback to make a throw without having to throw over, under, or between a defender. A quarterback with the physical ability to put touch on the ball and mental awareness when to use touch are invaluable. As such, it is important not to eliminate the kid with the not-so-strong arm when evaluating your quarterback talent pool.

Discovering a quarterback with touch can sometimes be more valuable to you in the long run than the quarterback that comes out the first day of practice and wows everybody with his rocket arm, but fails to put touch on the ball. This is not to say that he can't learn how to put touch on the ball, but he will continue to try to throw the ball through defenders until you break him of this habit. It is not as though he is intentionally trying to defy you. It is merely the fact that, up to this point, he has been able to complete passes without touch. The point is that, now that he is on the varsity, he will be required to use touch to get the ball into smaller windows than he has before.

Velocity

The great quarterback coaches will tell you there is a distinct difference between velocity and arm strength. The strong-armed quarterback can throw the football through a brick wall or launch it 85 yards. The quarterback with velocity is capable of throwing an over-the-middle 16-yard dig route between inside linebackers or an 18-yard sideline out just out of the reach of the corner. This quarterback has what you call "zip." He has the ability to throw the ball with enough velocity to get the ball into fast closing windows or away from breaking defenders. A quarterback with velocity doesn't need to throw the ball hard all the time. He throws the ball as hard as it needs to be thrown. It is kind of a form of touch discussed earlier but in reverse. Velocity is putting more on the ball rather than less. The key is: knowing when to use it. A quarterback may go an entire game and put real zip on the ball maybe half a dozen times, if that.

When you play good teams, the windows are smaller and defensive backs break faster. Having a quarterback that can deliver the ball with velocity and the touch necessary to drop the ball over defenders is optimal. What good is a quarterback that can zip the ball into windows 16 to 18 yards downfield, but can't make a touch throw over dropping linebackers, a back out of the backfield, or a simple swing pass? Having a quarterback that can throw with great velocity is only as good as the discretion he uses when utilizing his ability to throw the ball hard.

Some quarterbacks that can throw the ball with great velocity also share similar traits to the strong-armed quarterback discussed earlier. Some, but not all, have that ugly trait of trying to squeeze the ball into closed windows or thinking that they can throw the ball with enough velocity to go through a human being.

Trajectory

Trajectory is defined as "a path an object has through space." In this case, the ball is the object, and trajectory can be viewed as a combination of touch and velocity. A quarterback that understands trajectory has an innate ability to know what angle and speed is best and proper to get the ball into the wide receiver's hands. It is almost an unconscious feel that the quarterback possesses that allows him to know what angle of trajectory is necessary to put the ball over, under, and between defenders as well as make the ball catchable to a wide receiver on the run. It is a sixth sense the quarterback has that enables him to calculate the following:

- How fast the person he's throwing to is
- What direction (angle) he is heading
- If defenders are in the way

It is up to the quarterback to quickly analyze these three factors and put the correct trajectory on the ball. Some quarterbacks do this faster than others. If your quarterback doesn't grasp the concept of trajectory at first, it may be he needs more time practicing different throws to different wide receivers. The goal is for the quarterback and wide receiver to have a feel for what trajectory the ball will be coming from in the game.

❏ Examples of Trajectory

The Bomb

The best example of trajectory is the path that the quarterback puts the ball when he is throwing to a wide receiver who is running a deep fly route or the bomb. The quarterback must initially throw the ball at such an angle and depth that the ball will come down and arrive in the wide receiver's hands at a point downfield with the wide receiver running at full speed. A common phrase is: "Let the wide receiver run under it," meaning the quarterback's delivery is at a trajectory that he will throw the ball in front and over the wide receiver so he will catch up with the ball at a point downfield by running full speed. The key is to put the appropriate trajectory for the individual wide receiver. The speed of your wide receivers is different; thus, the trajectory used for each wide receiver is different. The faster the wide receiver, the more trajectory necessary. It goes against the laws of physics to try to throw a ball deep without "putting some air under it." It is impossible to tell the quarterback exactly how far to lead a wide receiver when throwing the bomb. The timing of this pattern and what trajectory to use can only be perfected with a lot of practice. Other subtleties also must be considered, such as making sure the bomb throw stays on the sideline away from inside defenders and is out of the reach of a cover defender as well. This all must be analyzed in a split second to determine what trajectory to use when throwing the ball deep. Practice, practice, practice.

The Out Route

The two types of out routes are essentially: speed cut or man cut. The speed cut is rounded about a yard or two prior to maximum depth so the receiver ends up going straight to the sideline at maximum depth. The man cut requires that the wide receiver get the defensive back on his inside hip while gaining depth, then breaking or separating from the defender toward the sideline at maximum depth. Both of these routes require much different trajectory than the bomb. The trajectory on this throw is much flatter. Whereas the bomb trajectory is high and rounded, the out route trajectory is low and straight. The out route is one of those throws that the quarterback can put a lot of zip on, as long as there is not a defender between him and his receiver. If there is a defender between himself and the wide receiver, the quarterback must adjust his trajectory so the ball goes over or around such defender. This is easier said than done when it comes to the quarterback having a feel for what trajectory is necessary to adjust to the speed and angle of his receiver as well as the position of the defense. Quarterback coaches use the phrase "throw it on a line," which means that the quarterback has the arm strength to throw the ball at a low height for a substantial distance. He doesn't need a lot of height on his throw because he possesses the strength and velocity to get the ball to travel a farther distance without a high trajectory.

❑ The All-Telling 18-Yard Out Route. How Much Trajectory?

One of the basic throws college and pro scouts use in evaluating a prospective quarterback is the deep comeback out at 18 yards. From this throw, they can get a pretty good idea of a quarterback's arm capability. The quarterback that can throw an 18-yard out without a high trajectory ("throw it on a line") probably has a pretty strong arm. Scouts want to see the ball come out of the quarterback's hand nice and flat on its way to the receiver. A quarterback who must put a high trajectory on an 18-yard out is bound to have the ball intercepted because the longer the ball is in the air the more time the defense has to react and defend the pass.

What scouts sometimes don't see is whether that quarterback who throws the 18-yard out "on a line" also has the *sense* to alter his trajectory based on a defender between himself and the receiver. Outside linebackers are coached to get under that deep out throw. Their assignment is a success if they force the quarterback to alter his trajectory on the out route. The more that outside linebacker can force the quarterback to put more air on his throw, the longer he has given his defensive back time to react. If the defense does a decent job of getting a defender under the 18-yard out route it doesn't mean that you can't still complete the pass. It may not be the absolute perfect pass to the wide receiver, but it should be catchable. Your quarterback may only throw the ball on a line four to six times in an entire game. The rest of his throws will require touch and proper trajectory. There are very few times during the course of a game that there is not a defender to deal with when throwing to a wide receiver.

The Seam Route

The seam route is run by a tight end, slotback, or running back. The route is predominantly run versus a two-safety secondary. If you have a wide receiver running a fade pattern and a tight end or running back running a seam pattern, you force the safety to decide who to cover. If the safety read takes you to the tight end, then you have inside linebackers to deal with. This throw needs to be placed under the safeties and over the linebackers. Touch and trajectory are essential. Throw the ball too high, and the safety picks it off. Throw the ball with no trajectory, and the linebackers get to it. The seam route throw is a true test of a quarterback's ability to determine what trajectory is necessary and the ability to execute it.

Foot Quickness

When talking about physical quickness and how it pertains to the quarterback, coaches generally think of foot quickness. The two best examples are Tom Brady and Peyton Manning. They are probably the two slowest straight distance runners in the NFL. You could time their 40-yard dash with an hourglass. Put them in the pocket, and it is a different story. They float around like a ballerina. It is no accident that they rarely get sacked. They have that innate ability to feel a pass rush coupled with the physical attribute of quick feet. You can see their feet moving while their vision is downfield. Some coaches call it "happy feet." I call it maintaining perfect balance while sorting things out downfield.

There is a big difference between being fast and having quick feet. Having a quarterback who can run fast is not a bad thing. A quarterback with good speed is capable of making big plays by scrambling, running the option, or pulling the ball down and gaining big yards on a broken play. A quarterback with quick feet is able to set himself in the pocket and maneuver just enough to buy time to deliver the ball. Very rarely in a game is a quarterback able to take his drop and have perfect protection from his offensive line. More times than not, he will be required to move around in the pocket to avoid the defensive rush. The ability to maneuver out of tight situations quickly is a great trait to have. It is a sense a quarterback has between his brain and his feet that allow him to find the little pockets inside the big pocket with quick movements of his feet. When drilling footwork, you want to emphasize the ball up at shoulder height. You don't want all that great footwork to go down the toilet because the ball was not in a position to be released.

Foot quickness is something that you can help develop in your quarterback. Two of the best drills to do with your quarterback are the ladder drill and the wave drill. The wave drill is good for pure foot quickness. Training dropback muscles to fire fast and often are accomplished with the ladder drill (Figure 1-7).

Figure 1-7. Ladder drill

The next drill incorporates a visual cue with foot quickness. The quarterback takes his prescribed drop, then floats quickly in the pocket based on the coach pointing in different directions. The quarterback must maintain good ball positioning with his eyes downfield while he changes direction. Figure 1-8 shows the coach pointing in a backward, forward, left, and right direction. Once the coach gets the quarterback to a set position, he can signal left, right, forward, backward, duck, spin, jump, or anything else you can think of. Have a coach with a broom badger the passer. The drill finishes with the coach giving the quarterback a direction to escape. The quarterback escapes or takes off in one direction with his eyes downfield and the ball in a throwing set. Once he defines his receiver, the quarterback squares his shoulders to the target and throws on the run. The first two to three steps of the escape are the most important. The quarterback must feel what it's like to escape, get away, before thinking about throwing. You can mix in all sorts of different things for your quarterback to do.

Figure 1-8. Wave drill

Side note: Once a quarterback has escaped the pocket, either by designed sprint pass or ad libbing, a right-handed quarterback will always push off his right foot to throw whether he is rolling right or left. A lefty will push off his left.

The wave and ladder drill is another good way to combine foot quickness and visual cues (Figure 1-9).

Figure 1-9. Wave and ladder drill

Vision

Vision may be the most important trait a quarterback can possess. Please refer to Chapter 2 to examine ways to help your quarterback develop vision and confidence. All of the quarterback traits mentioned in this chapter are important, but none more than vision. A quarterback that can see the field and know what he seeing is valuable. It is not easy to analyze what you are seeing downfield while color and humanity occur around you in the pocket. A quarterback that can make sense of what is happening downfield when everything is moving around him is special. It takes courage and guts to stand in the pocket while keeping your vision and focus downfield surveying the defense. Rare is the quarterback who will stand in the pocket to the last second before releasing the pass. Many quarterbacks feel pressure and lose their vision downfield.

> *"The quarterback is like an artist. The artist controls what goes where on the canvas. The quarterback controls what goes where on the gridiron. His focus is on his receivers downfield and the on-rushers become a swirl of colors beneath the main vision."*
>
> —Steve Clarkson

Don't Ask Your Young Quarterback to See Too Much

As a coach, you can help your quarterback's vision by not asking him to see too much. Help him by giving him "one-man" reads initially. His vision is limited through no fault of his own. He just lacks the experience of finding the open wide receiver through all of the movement and chaos in front of him. Give him a chance to enjoy some success before you ask him to execute the more complicated reads. Roll him out, run play-action, but don't put your young quarterback in difficult situations by asking him to consistently sit in the pocket, face a rush, and see the field like you want him to. You must facilitate good quarterback vision by calling plays that change his launch points. By differing where the quarterback is releasing the ball, you allow your young quarterback to have better vision and in turn he will make good decisions and complete passes.

What Affects Quarterback Vision?

- *Fear.* Your quarterback might not be mentally or physically strong. Maybe your quarterback is overwhelmed with his situation. He was okay with practice, but it's game time now, and he is petrified. This is not the time for you to drop him deep into the pocket and expect him to have clear and concise vision. It is now necessary for you to get him some rhythm in the game by calling plays that don't require a great deal looking and analyzing. Have him sprint to a one-man route to get him some good vision and complete a pass. Give him a chance to acclimate himself to the speed and tempo of the game before stretching his capabilities.

- *He is unsure of what he's doing.* Even though he has overcome his fear, it all seems a garble because he doesn't have a clue what he's looking at. He doesn't know who he is reading, so his vision is all over the place. He has 20/20 eyesight, but his football vision is blind.

- *He is unsure that his receivers know what they are doing.* When a quarterback is not 100 percent sure that his wide receivers will get to their assigned spots, he unconsciously strays from the defender he is supposed to read trying to find the wide receiver he is looking for.

- *He lacks confidence in his offensive line.* A quarterback that lacks confidence in his offensive line will go into survival mode. If he has had to scramble the last four times he has dropped back, then he is going to be more concerned with his physical well-being than completing a pass. His vision will not be downfield reading the secondary coverage. His vision will be focused on the ugly guys rushing in, trying to cause him great bodily harm.

- *His physical stature.* Being shorter affects vision. A short quarterback does not see the middle of the field as well as he sees the perimeter. Too much is happening directly in front of him, which obstructs his sight to the middle of the formation. This is not to say that a short quarterback cannot throw over the middle. A few short quarterbacks have a gift of being able to see through, around, and under the rush to find their receivers. They are rare. Assume that you are going to have to develop a passing game that helps the quarterback's vision by giving him plays that allow him to get out around that rush. As he gains more experience, start taking his eyes to the middle of the field.

Accuracy

The quarterback that can throw the ball precisely where it needs to be is a valuable commodity. He may have good vision and a strong arm, but if he lacks accuracy the ball will wind up on the ground or worse yet in the defender's hands. Taking into account the many variables that come into play when throwing to a moving target and then having the physical ability to put the ball exactly where it needs to be is a gift. Accuracy does not mean it is a perfect throw. Accuracy is placing the ball where it needs to be to complete the pass. Sometimes this will entail throwing the ball out of the reach of the defender but within reach of the receiver. The receiver may have to stretch or even dive for the ball but the ball is out of the reach of the defender and catchable to the receiver. This is an accurate throw. Accuracy combines a few of the quarterback traits discussed earlier. Arm strength, release, touch, velocity, and the like all pertain to accuracy. Sometimes the ball needs to be thrown far, short, soft, hard, over, under, or between defenders. Very simply put, accuracy is the ability to deliver the ball precisely where desired and necessary.

Quarterback Intangibles

Intangibles cannot be measured with a scale or yardstick. They are characteristics that are impossible to quantify but obviously present.

Mental Quickness

Quickness takes on different meanings when it comes to quarterbacking. Yes, being physically quick is an important trait to have, but when it comes to the quarterback, other forms of quickness are essential if he is going to be able to avoid a rush or evade a tackle. More important than physical quickness is mental quickness. Anybody who has ever sat in the pocket can tell you that the ability to see, analyze, and react quickly is absolutely necessary. Being mentally quick entails performing various different mental tasks in a short period of time. Much of the timing that comes to mind when talking about quarterbacks is the mental clock that occurs when the quarterback drops back to pass. A quarterback that possesses a mental clock when dropping back in the pocket has a good idea as to when the pocket will collapse or his receivers are not going to get open. He will have a feel for when his time to throw the ball has run out and he must either get rid of it or escape. Some quarterbacks will escape too quickly because they feel like they can see better outside. They feel more comfortable running away from the enemy rather than standing in the pocket and trusting their offensive line; they tried that. They don't have to stand in the pocket and make sense of the garble they see directly in front of them.

Help Your Quarterback Develop a Mental Clock

A quarterback that does not develop a mental clock in the pocket will drive you crazy. He will escape when guys are wide open and/or stand in the pocket and get sacked when he should have delivered the ball. As the coach, you must do everything you can during practice and drills to help the quarterback establish a mental clock. The mental clock should jibe perfectly with the specific footwork inherent to the play. You can't ask the quarterback to get rid of the ball quickly when you ask him to take a five-step drop. Remember how Joe Montana used to drop back, set his feet, and very rhythmically go through his read progression. His clock was so precise that he knew exactly when to go from one potential receiver to another so that, by the time the protection broke down, the ball was delivered and the receiver was getting yards-after-carry. He knew exactly how long he could stay focused on one receiver before he had to go to another, and then another. His mental clock was perfectly coordinated with his drop. His clock started from the time he took the snap from the center to the time he delivered. He knew precisely, based on his footwork, how long he could take to see everything he needed to see then get the heck out of the pocket. Developing a mental clock with your quarterback takes into account the drop, set, routes being run, and protection. A quarterback without a clock is a disaster.

Think Quickly, But Don't Rush

There is a big difference between thinking quickly in the pocket and feeling rushed. An experienced quarterback knows that things will be happening quickly when he drops into a pocket. This is no surprise. Defensive line players are rushing him with reckless abandon, linebackers are either dropping into their pass responsibilities or blitzing, and defensive backs are executing coverages. All of this is happening very quickly, and it is up to the quarterback to analyze all of that in a split second and deliver the ball. You, the coach, can help your quarterback develop mental quickness.

Use Visualization

One of the best exercises quarterbacks can do to improve their mental quickness is visualization. The mind does not know the difference between reality and imagination. One of the most productive drills you can perform with your quarterback is to have him shut his eyes, give him a play, and have him imagine running that play at game tempo. Require that he imagine or visualize literally everything. Have him visualize getting the play signal, communicating with his offensive team, going through the cadence while surveying the defense (pre-snap read), feeling the ball being snapped into his hands, executing the proper drop for the play, reading the appropriate defender, and last but not least, delivering a perfect throw. The perfect throw may require any of the variables discussed earlier: zip, touch, velocity, and the like. Require that your quarterback verbalize what he is visualizing, allowing you to check, correct, or reinforce what he is seeing mentally. Ask your quarterback what specific defenders are doing on each play.

By requiring that your quarterback verbalize what he is visualizing, you can be certain he is reading the correct defender for each play.

A Fun Visualization Exercise

When I played quarterback in college, I would have dinner with my wide receiver coach John Crivello and his family every Wednesday night during the season. John's wife Kathy was a great cook, and John was a passing game genius. By Wednesday of game week, the game plan was pretty much set. After dinner, John and I would retire to the hot tub, where he would, based on the game plan, give me the down-and-distance, play, front, and coverage for every conceivable scenario we might see on Saturday. I would play the game in my mind. This was done in rapid-fire fashion. We would run the same play with different down-and-distances and different coverages. If we were going to play a night game, I would play the game mentally under the lights. If it was a day game, I visualized that. Every possible combination of game situations would be posed to me at an extremely quick pace. I was practicing to be mentally quick. I could literally play a complete game mentally in about 15 minutes.

This approach is a way to get hundreds of mental reps in during your week of preparation. You don't have to do it for 15 minutes. You can play an entire game mentally, or just one play. It can be done anywhere. The key to learning is repetition. It only follows that the more reps your mind gets, the faster and more efficient it will be.

Decision Making

Quick and accurate decision making comes as a result of proper preparation. Asking your quarterback to make quick decisions without arming him with the mental tools to do so is unfair. It is difficult to ascertain whether your quarterback is capable of quick decision making until he is put in a position to think and react quickly. Proper decision making is crucial when a quarterback must make split-second choices that directly affect the outcome of the game. Your quarterback is in the best position of anyone else on the field to screw it up. His decision making can determine winning or losing. Other players can make minor mistakes during the course of a game, and no one is any worse for the wear, but when your quarterback makes a minor mistake, it could have catastrophic consequences.

Your quarterback must not be a selfish person when it comes to his decision making. He must realize that his choices affect the entire team, not just him. His decision making must be based on what is best for the team and not himself. Quarterbacks who are more concerned with personal stats tend to be poor decision makers. Decisions become based on what is best for him and not the team.

Your quarterback's decision making ability is tested when he:
- Is given the freedom to observe what the defense is giving him at the line of scrimmage and make calls and checks
- Gets a pre-snap read and decides where his post-snap focus will be centered
- Reads the reaction of the defense to his pass route and decides which receiver is likely to be open
- Decides whether his receiver is actually open or not (This is often the subject of debate.)
- Makes the correct decision as to who to throw to
- Makes the decision to throw to a covered receiver or not
- Decides what to do once he determines he is not going to throw to a covered receiver

Throw the Ball Away, or "Force It"

The most important choice a quarterback could potentially make during a game is whether to force the ball to a covered receiver or not. Once a quarterback has gone through his read progression and determines he has no receiver open, he has three choices:
- Throw the ball to the covered receiver, and risk interception.
- Tuck the ball, and make the best of it.
- Throw the ball away.

You can help your quarterback as well as the team by assuring your quarterback that it is okay to throw the ball away or pull it down and run. You want to "live another down." Only in rare, specific instances should you force the ball. Reinforce his good judgment when he shows good restraint. Do it in front of the team so everybody understands why the quarterback will throw an incomplete pass now and then.

Even professional quarterbacks with tremendous decision making ability occasionally force the ball into bad situations because the temptation to make something out of nothing is too great. Good decision making takes discipline as well as good judgment. If you reward the quarterback enough times, he won't be reluctant to do the right thing.

"Throw it into the fifth row"

I was coaching quarterbacks at Northern Arizona University. I worked with a talented, coachable, and smart quarterback named Scott Lindquist. One day, at an outside practice, in an attempt to make him comfortable throwing the ball away, I used the phrase "Throw the ball into the fifth row." I wanted to let him know that it was just fine with me if he threw the ball away when his receivers were covered and it was double okay to throw it *way* away. I would tell Scott, "Sometimes we may not call the perfect play. Don't make a bad play a terrible play. Throw the ball away. We've got other plays that'll work."

Our indoor stadium had bleachers that literally hang over the field. During a home game that fall Scott dropped back into the pocket and found no receivers open. He scrambled, ran all over the place, and then proceeded to throw the ball in a way and direction that left an indelible image on my brain. It was the most side-armed, no-look, get-rid-of-it throw these eyes have ever witnessed. The ball sailed over every player on the field and proceeded to land in the fifth row. When Scott came to the sideline, I asked, "What was that?" He said, "You told me that sometimes you make a bad call, and I am not to make your bad call a terrible call by forcing it. You also told me to 'Throw it into the fifth row.' Coach, that was the worst call you've ever made, so I threw the ball into the fifth row." We both busted up laughing! It was a terrible call, so he literally threw the ball into the fifth row!

Anticipation

Anticipation takes various forms when it comes to quarterbacking. A quarterback that can anticipate where a defender will be or go is more likely to make his read quicker and more efficiently. The quarterback who can anticipate where and when his receiver will break open is more apt to deliver the ball before his protection breaks down or the defensive backs can react to his throw. Anticipation is a sense of alertness and understanding that allows a quarterback to more easily predict the occurrence of events that start at the snap of the ball and end when the whistle is blown. The ability to anticipate can only occur when there is a thorough knowledge of why and how all of the different parts react to each other. For example: your quarterback will have difficulty anticipating what the strong safety is going to do in cover 3 when you send a back to the flat if he doesn't have an understanding of cover 3 and what the strong safety's duties are. When he knows that the strong safety is responsible for the flat in cover 3, he can anticipate him covering the back in the flat. If you place another receiver in the space vacated by that cover 3 safety, then he will be open. If the quarterback has a feel for all this, then he will anticipate the strong safety biting on the back and deliver the ball to the open receiver in a smooth unrushed manner. The quarterback's anticipation of what the strong safety was going to do is based on sound, technical knowledge gained prior to the event.

Based on this knowledge, the quarterback can anticipate events that will aid in the execution of the play. He will be able to anticipate who will react to what and subsequently make quick, accurate decisions. Quicker and more accurate because the quarterback anticipated what was going to happen based on prior knowledge. Memorizing pass routes is not enough. Anticipation occurs when the quarterback has a sense of how all the parts react to each other.

Leadership

> *"Leadership must be demonstrated, not announced."*
>
> —Fran Tarkenton

The best leaders lead by example. Your quarterback should be the first one out to practice and the last one to leave. He should be the most coachable player on the field. His leadership should transcend the field of play and rub off on his teammates, on and off the gridiron. A quarterback leads with body language, tone of voice, enthusiasm, attention to detail, and effort.

Enthusiasm

> *"ENTHUSIASM is the fire in our furnace, it is the spark that keeps us going in high gear. It makes going great.*
>
> *Enthusiasm brings on Excitement*
>
> *Excitement then produces Energy*
>
> *Energy generates Extra Effort*
>
> *Extra effort develops Excellence"*
>
> —Frosty Westering

A quarterback's enthusiasm is contagious. When a quarterback is enthusiastic about the process as well as the product, he raises the energy level of the entire team. There is no better position on a football team than the quarterback to display and invoke enthusiasm. Offensive linemen especially appreciate it when their quarterback gets fired up. They play a violent game up front. They like to know that their quarterback has a kick-ass attitude!

Being enthusiastic does not mean loud. Your quarterback does not need to be vocal to be a good leader. Teammates follow the person who sets a good example. Actions speak louder than words when it comes to leading from the quarterback position. Although the quarterback is viewed as "special" he is just one of eleven guys. He can lead best by getting *his* job done. No more, no less. The best way a quarterback can lead is by doing what he is supposed to do on a consistent basis. The quarterback that yells at teammates but doesn't take care of his own business will not be viewed as a leader. The quarterback that is selfish by forcing the ball when he should throw it away will not be a leader very long. He can't expect to lead when he can't do his own job.

Mental Toughness

"Our mistakes don't make or break us. If we are lucky, they simply reveal who we really are, what we're really made of."

—Donn Moomaw

Being able to bounce back from a mistake is critical in the life of a quarterback. Unlike any other position on the field, the quarterback's mistakes are obvious to everyone. If the right guard makes a mistake, nobody knows but his mom and dad. A quarterback that responds to adversity in a positive way will not only improve his performance in the future, he will also be an example to his teammates. The offensive line and wide receivers don't want to see their quarterback at the end of the bench, sulking after a mistake.

"If you want to see a fighter at his best, watch him when he is getting beat."

—Sugar Ray Robinson

The mental toughness of the quarterback will motivate his teammates. How many times have you heard a player describe how motivating it was to him to watch his quarterback take a beating but keep doing his job. Offensive linemen will fight for a quarterback that understands that sacks happen. They don't appreciate a quarterback who dramatizes his mistakes. The ironic thing is it might not have been a blocking breakdown at all. The quarterback's failure to do his job may have caused the sack.

Accepting tough coaching and responding with confidence are signs of mental toughness. Being receptive to honest criticism in the heat of battle is extra difficult. Making a mistake and then accepting immediate criticism is tough. It takes a tough-minded person to accept tough coaching. Tough coaching doesn't mean belittling or unconstructive criticism. It means being the one person in this football world who is going to tell it like it is. As long as your quarterback understands that you have his best interest in mind, he will understand why you are tough on him and subsequently will become tougher himself.

Work Habits

"You become your choices. Your choices become habits. Make good choices and you develop good habits."

—Shambe Wright-Fair

Your quarterback should be the hardest worker on your team. His hard work serves both himself and the team. The quarterback gains the benefits of his time and effort while he serves as an example to his teammates. The quarterback's work ethic is visible for all to see. When the players see him as the first person out to practice and the last to leave, they gain respect for him. When they witness the quarterback attempting to perfect his craft, they are compelled to do the same.

The following quarterback work habits can improve a team in many ways:
- Spending extra time in film analysis with his coach analyzing opponents' tendencies
- Meeting with his coaches to clarify game plans
- Getting an extra set or more reps in the weight room; performing quarterback-specific lifts
- Perfecting routes with all wide receivers after practice
- Taking extra snaps from the centers
- Refining pitches and handoffs to running backs
- Performing quarterback-specific ball drills
- Performing surgical tubing stretches and exercises to strengthen and maintain flexibility
- Having a ball in his hands while watching TV (The ball must become an extension of the quarterback's hand.)
- Squeezing wrist grippers and/or performing wrist exercises to help him grip the ball better

The best thing a quarterback can do for himself and his team is to perfect his own game first, *then* do all he can to make everyone around him better.

Facing Adversity

> *"Man's greatest moment of happiness is to be tested beyond what he thought might be his breaking point and not fail."*
>
> —Joseph Murphy

How your quarterback reacts to adversity will be one of the most important factors in the success of your team. His ability to function when the chips are down will be necessary if he is to overcome the many challenges presented to him over the course of a season, game, or play.

How your quarterback reacts to an interception, a fumble, being behind, a failed third-down attempt, and such will affect both himself and the team. As a coach, you would like to see a happy medium. You don't want to see your quarterback fall apart emotionally, but you would like to see a small bit of remorse. You would like to know that he is at least aware of his mistake(s). Subsequently, you want to see him put it behind him and look to the future. An ability to accept the present situation, examine solutions, and continue to fight is what you would like to see from your quarterback.

"Put your information across slowly and repeat it over and over again! Take a difficult point and make it so simple that it will become clear to even the dullard."

—Knute Rockne

Help Your Young Quarterback Gain Confidence

How you handle the young, inexperienced quarterback could determine the difference between a great season and a highly frustrating one. All coaches have encountered the situation of trying to groom a young, first-time quarterback at the varsity level. What makes it more difficult at times is the fact that your previous quarterback may have been a senior starter that you had a great deal of confidence in and was able to execute nearly every play in the playbook.

They're All Different

Every new quarterback is different. First of all, his general knowledge of the varsity offensive playbook is not great, his skill level may be different, his strengths might not be the same, and last but not least his maturity level may be significantly different. Your new quarterback may have run the same system at the lower levels, but his grasp of the faster game as well as all the concepts and skills necessary to execute your varsity offense may not yet be developed. You are doing your young quarterback as well as your offensive team a disservice if you, the coach, make things more difficult for him than it already is. Don't ask him to make reads and/or perform techniques that he is not ready to do.

A Smart Off-Season

It is tempting to expand your offensive attack with meticulous research in the off-season. It's commendable that you want to expand and improve, but be careful when you expand on a scheme that your young quarterback hasn't a clue of. It's tough to not do things offensively that you feel will help your team. The "great expansion" may have to wait a year or so. Scheming and diagramming in the off-season is worthless if your quarterback can't execute it. All those clinics and research is only as good as your ability to perform it. Don't waste time and energy researching plays and skills that your quarterback (team) will be incapable of performing in the fall.

He Can Do *Something*

A lot of different offensive systems can work. Each system requires a unique quarterback skill set. The SNH attack offers the coach a variety of different options for the quarterback based on his distinct competence. Whether your quarterback is a better runner or passer, you have choices. If your quarterback is a better passer than runner, many things can be done in the sprint, screen, play-action, quick, and dropback passing game. If you have a good offensive line, it really doesn't matter. With a great offensive line, you can do a little or a lot of both passing and running. You can limit what the quarterback is asked to do while continuing to effectively move the ball.

With the SNH, there is no reason to feel like your offensive attack is doomed just because your quarterback lacks some of the abilities you would like to see. The SNH not only gives you balance between run and pass, but also balance between which players handle the ball. With some creativity and a little common sense, it is perfectly feasible to run an SNH attack without a multi-talented quarterback.

It is up to you to ask your young quarterback to do things that he will be successful at and not necessarily things you would like and/or planned to do. It is important to realize that every player is different in some way. Your new quarterback may have similar traits as your last quarterback, but he is different in some way. His strengths may not jibe with the talent you have at the other position groups, or maybe his skill level is so limited that you need to drastically rethink your play selection. Whatever it is, do not ask him to do things he can't do just because your last quarterback could do them.

Every Year Is Different

Quarterbacks come with varying skill sets every year. Every quarterback is unique. Don't force a young and/or inexperienced quarterback to adapt to your entire system. It is not the quarterback who needs to adapt; it is the coach. Spend time working on those skills in which the quarterback is deficient, but it is the coach who must evaluate the quarterback not so much to determine what to do but what not to do. You are not going to throw the SNH out merely because your quarterback is limited physically, mentally, or emotionally. It's not fair to him or the team to scrap a great offensive scheme just because he can't execute the entire playbook. Evaluate what your quarterback is best at, and use those skills within your existing system. He may not be able to do it all, but you won't be setting you and your quarterback up for failure by asking him to do things of which he is incapable.

You Have Options

The SNH offers a myriad of options for the coach who must determine a plan of attack based on his quarterback's talents and/or shortcomings. The spread no-huddle attack is so diverse, chances are he will be able to do something. If it takes eliminating certain plays or techniques from your playbook, then do so. You may find that once he has mastered the simplified version of your offense, he will gradually be able to do more. Recognize what his strong points are as early as you can, and emphasize those as soon as you can. By introducing the scheme one piece at a time and matching those pieces to your young quarterback's strengths and abilities, you give him a chance to grasp the X's and O's while enjoying success and gaining confidence. If given too much too early, he will not understand what he is doing. He will experience failure, which will cause him and the team to lose confidence.

Help Him Blossom

You will be amazed at how quickly and far your young quarterback will progress during the course of the season if you take a smart and limited approach to how you introduce the varsity offense to him. You must give him plays that maximize his physical ability and mental capacity. If it takes dumbing down your offensive playbook, then do so. You would much rather have him try and possibly fail at something he is capable of doing than frustrate the both of you by asking too much of him. He will lose the confidence necessary to improve. His teammates will sense this and lose confidence in him as well, which is a recipe for disaster. One of the most gratifying feelings a quarterback coach can have is watching a young/inexperienced quarterback progress from mastering the basic elements of the SNH system to the full gambit of checks, audibles, sight adjusts, and plays.

Vision Is Key

Vision of the field is probably hardest thing for a young quarterback. Vision does not refer to his eyesight measurement, such as 20/20 or 20/30. It refers to his ability to see defenders and execute his assignment while in the pocket or on the move. Your young quarterback may have 20/20 eyesight, but lack vision when the ball is snapped. Some quarterbacks have it, and some don't. Some quarterbacks can read a defense with no problem when they are in a 7-on-7 drill, but totally flustered when you put a rushing defensive line in front of them. Most young quarterbacks need time to develop the vision necessary to execute an intricate offensive passing scheme. It's not their fault. They just don't have the experience.

Don't make it more difficult for him than it already is. It is a fact that the higher the level of play, the faster the game is played. It takes time for the young quarterback to adjust to the speed of the varsity game as well as learn the new terms and assignments that you are throwing at him. Come to grips with the fact that his field vision may not be as advanced as a seasoned, experienced quarterback. Find out what his strengths are, and coach the heck out of him.

Quarterback vision on the football field is affected by a variety of factors. In order to have field vision, the quarterback should have a firm grasp of the following:

- Where his receivers are lined up in the formation and why
- The concepts of vertical and horizontal stretch in pass play design
- An intuitive feel for the physical and mental capabilities of his receivers
- What defense he sees and an educated guess as to how they will react to the play that's called
- His judgment of the abilities of his offensive linemen
- His judgment of the abilities of the defense he is facing
- His own limitations and willingness to expose himself to physical harm
- The confidence he has in the coach's play call
- The down-and-distance situation he faces
- The obvious difficulty of seeing downfield while a blur of color and motion are taking place in his line of sight
- The pressure associated with a critical game situation (e.g., desperation two-minute drill, fourth down at the end of the game, etc.)

Many factors contribute to how your young quarterback is going to see the field after the ball is snapped. Many of these factors are not necessarily conscious thoughts, but they do influence his vision.

Help Your Young Quarterback Enjoy Some Rhythm and Success

Don't make life more difficult for your young quarterback by asking him to drop back deep in the pocket and make multiple reads. Sprint-out and play-action passes are two things you can ask him to do that will give him the confidence to perform more challenging tasks as he gains confidence. Don't ask your young quarterback to perform reads and techniques that you asked your senior starter last fall. First of all, his field vision may not be as advanced as last year's seasoned, experienced quarterback, and secondly he may not have a suitable mental grasp of what you are asking. Get him in the rhythm of the game by calling plays he has shown he can run. By calling plays that he has displayed an ability to perform, you facilitate success. This success will serve to increase your quarterback's confidence as well as show the rest of the team that their quarterback knows what he is doing.

Be Realistic: Put Yourself in His Cleats

It is amazing to watch major college and pro quarterbacks put the ball into such tight windows while they have Godzillas aggressively rushing them. It is amusing to see a person who has never played the quarterback position go berserk in front of their television when the quarterback doesn't make a perfect throw or does not see an open receiver. How would that person react to dropping into an NFL pocket and trying to recognize an open receiver? The first thing that would overcome him is fear. Fear of the huge grown men in helmets and protective gear that are paid to annihilate them. The second is vision. He would probably be so overcome with fear that looking for an open receiver is the last thing on his mind. The third is the physical ability to overcome the first two while throwing the ball to a moving target precisely between the secondary defenders.

What a Difference a Pass Rush Makes

Those coaches who have never been a quarterback must base their judgment solely on observing your quarterback's performance. Be careful. If your only judgment of him occurs during the summer months when your are participating in 7-on-7 passing drills, then you will not get a realistic feel for how your young quarterback will react to a pass rush. All quarterbacks do not react the same when you put a defensive line rush in front of them. He may have performed admirably in the 7-on-7 drills over the summer, but that doesn't necessarily mean he will perform the same when you put a pass rush in front of them. Assume that your young quarterback will need some time in the fall to acclimate himself to an aggressive pass rush as well as the increased speed of the varsity game. You can help him by being realistic when it comes to things you will ask him to do when he puts the pads on.

Work With His Skill Set, Not Your Mindset

Do not be one of those coaches who is so set in his ways that you will spend endless hours of time and instruction with your young quarterback, attempting to execute plays because you think your "great coaching" will be enough for him to be able to perform at your level of expectations. That approach is not fair to him or the team. It is wiser to spend practice time perfecting his skill set. Watch his face light up and his body language improve as he begins to enjoy success doing the realistic things that you ask him to do.

Sprint-Out and Play-Action Passes May Help Your Quarterback's Vision

Sprint-out and play-action passes are two things you can ask your quarterback to do until he gains the confidence to perform more challenging tasks. He will love you for not asking him to sit in the pocket and try to make reads while a blur of color and humanity fight it out at his feet. Even if his strength is not throwing on the run, he will probably be more successful throwing on the run because he will be able to see things better. Your young quarterback will appreciate the fact that he is running away from the chaos of the line of scrimmage and can focus downfield rather than be preoccupied with the defensive rush. Field vision is probably the hardest skill with which a young quarterback must deal.

If you really want to make it easy for your young quarterback, you will have him sprint to a single receiver and either throw the ball to him if he is open, or throw the ball out-of-bounds if he is covered. This approach is very simplistic, but it may be a good starting point for a young quarterback who lacks the vision and/or courage to pass from the pocket and/or the ability to read a defender before deciding where to throw.

The play shown in Figure 2-1 illustrates how the quarterback can roll to a single wide receiver and throw if he is open, look to a dragging wide receiver as a second choice, or throw the ball out-of-bounds.

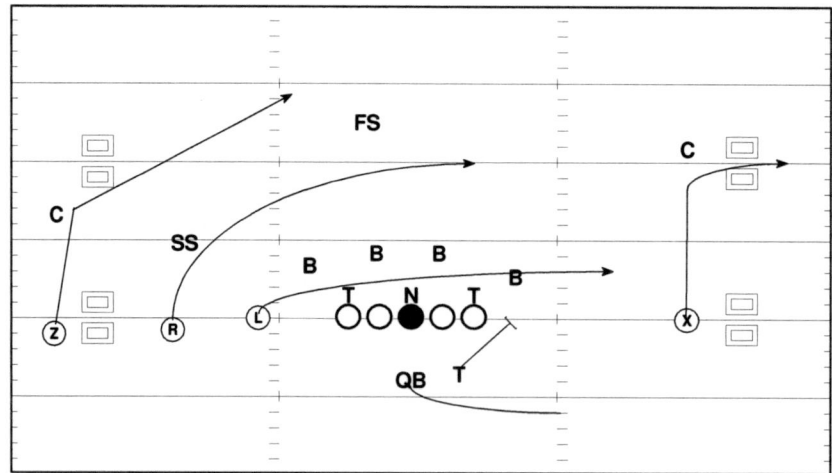

Figure 2-1. Phil 60 choice route

The play shown in Figure 2-2 illustrates a bootleg action that shows the defense a typical zone run-action tied to a bunch flood route. It incorporates the simple run-action footwork for the quarterback combined with sprint-action to three wide receivers flooding the wideside of the field. This helps the quarterback escape the rush while giving him a clean look at three possible receivers.

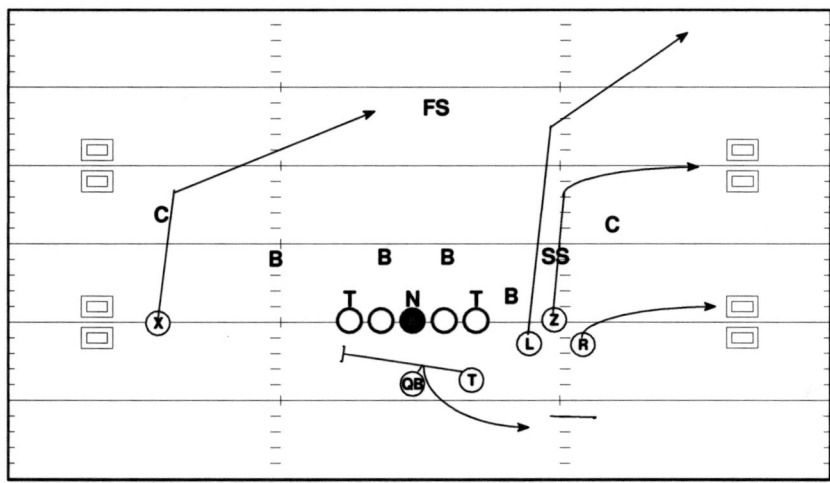

Figure 2-2. Bunch 225 ladder

Don't be alarmed if you ran the SNH last year and threw the ball a ton and you now find yourself this year with a quarterback who can't throw the ball past the line of scrimmage. With the SNH attack, you have options.

"When you find your opponent's weak spot, hammer it."

—John Heisman

Attack Defensive Weaknesses

He's There—You Just Have to Find Him

Every defensive team has a weakness. It might be the scheme they run or the personnel they possess. It might be the entire position group of defensive linemen, linebackers, defensive backs, or one or two particular individuals. It is rare to find a defensive group that doesn't have some kind of weakness, physically or schematically. It is up to you to find it and exploit it.

Defenses Are Evolving

Today's defenses are becoming much more creative in their approach to the SNH offense. The latest trends in defensive football are designed to defend the SNH with as few weaknesses as possible. Finding the defensive vulnerability is not as easy as in the past because many teams are playing with one less lineman and more hybrid players that are positioned for and physically capable of executing both run and pass assignments. You see defenses designed to stop both pass and run equally, pushing the boundaries of players in the box to defend run yet in a position to defend the pass. Blitzes and stunts are occurring every play from every angle. The 3-5 stack and 3-4 defenses are essentially 5-2 defensive linemen with 4-4 linebackers.

A Solid Defensive Approach

The new multi-linebacker, three-down-linemen defenses that can attack an SNH offense from multiple angles is a formidable approach. It is a great combination of defensive run and pass schemes. Defensive line gap and rush lane responsibilities as well as defensive back man and zone assignments are all sound and can be varied easily. Many smaller teams like the three-lineman front because it requires one less defensive lineman. Most small schools have an abundance of defensive backs and linebackers. It's hard to find big, strong guys.

The weakness in new five-linebacker defenses designed to stop the SNH may be the outside or inside linebacker who is being asked to fill a run gap/lane that he is not capable of. Defenses are getting better at reducing the amount of players that must perform completely different assignments when defending 21 personnel one week and 10 personnel the next.

Manipulate to Get What You Want

It is wise to script (mentally or in writing) formations that you begin a game with. Your first formation could expose a weakness, or it could take the entire game to figure out. He is out there. Maybe it will take getting lined up in a specific formation and then shifting and/or motioning to get you to your optimal mismatch between your best player against the defense's weakness. Whatever you can do to put your players in a better chance to succeed is the goal. You need flexibility in your terminology that allows you to shift, move, motion, freeze, and manipulate as many players as possible with a minimum amount of words.

You Have Answers!

Regardless of what defense you see, the SNH offense has ways of isolating and attacking defenders that are not equipped to do what they are being asked to do. Certain defensive players are better at some things than others. With the SNH, you are capable of attacking from all areas of the field. You have inside and outside run as well as various ways to throw the ball to an assortment of many different receivers.

Facilitate Effective Communication

Get creative. Yes, you may be adding a new term or phrase for a different shift or motion that is special to that week, but once implemented it could pay huge dividends. Invent one- or two-word play calls that tell many players at the same time. By packing a punch into every word in the play call, you are able to do all the shifting, motioning, and such with a minimal amount of words and syllables. By varying your disguise, you can run the same basic plays that have been your staple, but do it by manipulating the defense in such a way that you are executing your best plays against the defense's weakest player or have gained a one- or two-man advantage at the point of attack. Your players will pick up the new terminology or formations. If practiced and repped appropriately during the week, your players will be ready. A period of practice should be dedicated to practicing the execution of shifts and motions. The offensive linemen do not need to be present at the shift/motion period. They will be busy practicing their drills and fundamentals while the wide receivers and running backs are practicing ways to disguise or manipulate the defense in order to gain small advantages.

Expose and Isolate

One simple technique that can be used if you have a wide receiver that is head and shoulders more talented than the rest is to have a plan going into the game where the coach signals a switch call before a formation. This call tells the talented player to switch or match up with the defense's weak link. By throwing one word ("switch") into the call, you have told your most talented player to line up on their least talented player. Instant mismatch! Maybe the defense has a plan to man-up bump-and-run your best wide receiver. Merely line your best wide receiver up off the ball and have him motion into the spot he needs to be pre-snap, giving him a running head start to beat any tight man-to-man coverage or run away from an inferior defender.

At this point, you don't need new plays. The only thing you are doing as an offensive coach is taking all of the great technique you have taught, and are good at, and utilizing it against your opponent to its maximum effect. By isolating your more talented players versus your opponent's inferior personnel, you supercharge plays you already have. This is done by simply lining up your best against their worst or using one-word calls that shift or motion players to advantageous positions. You can run all of the plays that have been successful for you against the opponent's weakest player(s).

Same Guy, Different Defense

The player who was the run-stopper defensive end in the coach's defense last year is still the same guy, but in this year's defense he may be a walk-off outside linebacker. How about the 3 technique tackle that moves to a 6 technique rush end just because the defensive coach went to a clinic in the off-season and discovered the perfect defense for the SNH. The player is still the same person mentally and physically, but because the design of the defense changed he is put into a position based on body type and not ability. In the defensive coach's mind, he may be the perfect player for that position when in reality this player lacks the tools necessary to execute the various assignments inherent to the defensive scheme. He may be put at that position simply because of what he looks like and no real feel for what the position entails. At the college and pro levels, you can recruit players that possess the appropriate body type and skill set necessary to perform specific tasks essential to their specialized position. This is not the case at the high school level. You have more potential for tweeners at the high school level. *Tweeners* are players that, because of their physicality or skill set, are not necessarily a skill player or interior line player. The defensive coach may not have a big pool to draw from when assigning players to crucial positions. He may do his best, but chances are that one of his players will be unable to execute his assignments on a consistent basis.

What Defense Will You See? Does It Matter?

Anticipating an opponent's defensive plan can be interesting. One of the difficulties that you may face when running a spread no-huddle offense is getting relevant scouting information. With the advent of computerized film exchange, it is easy to watch film anywhere on any device: computer, tablet, phone, Hudl. Access to scout film is instantaneous, and more teams are running the spread no-huddle (which helps). You may have a hard time trying to find another spread no-huddle team that is as diversified and potent as you will be. Your spread no-huddle attacks with both run and pass. Your offensive attack is not one-dimensional. You may have film of your opponent's defense defending the same formations you run, but that doesn't necessarily mean they'll defend you that way. Your balanced SNH attack has put your opponent's defensive coordinator in a very precarious position of *pick your poison*. It shouldn't matter what they run. You've got plenty of ways to exploit whatever they give you. Don't concern yourself all week worrying about precisely what defense you will see. If your players stick to their rules, it doesn't matter. You will pass the ball against a defense that's stacked up for the run and run the ball against a defense heavy in pass coverage.

What Is Their Base?

Most defenses stem from some sort of base. They like to stay in their base defensive front because that is what they know and are comfortable with. You can generalize and say that most defenses run a base defense that has a noseguard (odd) or not (even). From that point, defensive coaches do crazy things based on what their perception is of you. If they think they must stop the run first, you will see more defenders in the box. One of the biggest questions an offensive coach wants to answer as quickly as possible is: "What is the defense's plan? Are they going to cover or pressure?" If your perceived competence is throwing the ball, then you will see fewer players in the box to cover the pass or a bunch of guys in the box to put the heat on you. Odd defenses, those with a noseguard, will probably be odd against you, and even defenses, those without a noseguard, will remain even.

The most notable differences will occur with defensive ends, linebackers, and defensive backs. Defensive ends that were normally in a three-point stance may be asked to stand up and displace themselves in order to execute a run fit or pass zone. Outside linebackers may have to be involved in pass defense as strong safeties. Two-gap or 1 technique defensive linemen may be asked to fill gaps or rush lanes they are not accustomed to. Maybe it's a lineman who must play a shade or assignment he's not familiar with. Maybe it's a linebacker or defensive back who is assigned a different man to cover, zone to occupy, or a run fit to fill.

Identify the base defense, and anticipate what adjustments they will make to the spread four- or five-receiver set. As the defense adjusts from their base to defend the spread formation, there are usually one or two players that may be put in a precarious situation. The goal is to manipulate the defense in such a way that you cause them to execute techniques and/or assignments that are not second nature to them.

Don't Worry!

As a coach, you must not give your team the impression that they will not be prepared just because you haven't seen your opponent line up against an SNH attack like yours. The worst thing you could do is make your team feel unprepared for their opponent. Tell your offensive team that you will all be learning what they (your opponent) have in mind at the same time. They will find some humor in that as well as enter the game with supreme confidence that it doesn't matter what defense the opponent comes up with; they will attack it one way or another. You've got answers for anything they throw at you. Don't worry if you are not able to predict precisely what defense you will see on Friday night, and by all means, do not give your players the feeling that you are not prepared for your next opponent just because you have not seen them against a spread team such as yours. This may occur a number of times during the season. As long as your players stick with their rules, it doesn't matter what defense you will face. You'll have answers.

"What the hell are they running?"

The absolute ideal situation is when you begin a game and realize your opponent has come up with an entirely different and/or new defense just for you. You may have 11 fish out of water in this case. Sound absurd? It's happened. Although you have to commend the defensive coordinator for trying to figure a way to stop you, he has basically said that he has no confidence in his existing defense and would rather ask his players to play positions they have never played before than play the defense that got him killed last year. His logic is that putting his players in different alignments is going to be the answer, when in reality he is merely putting the same inferior players in spots they will probably perform worse because they are less familiar with their position and how to play it. You may be surprised for the first couple of offensive plays, but you will quickly catch on to what their plan is and attack it.

Weaknesses to Look For

The following are the types of defensive weaknesses to look for:
- *Inferior personnel:* This is simply a defensive player that lacks the mental or physical ability to perform the duty he is being asked to do. This type of player can be found in any position group: defensive linemen, defensive backs, or linebackers. Sometimes these players stick out like a sore thumb, and sometimes they begin to stand out as you watch more film. Just like your own team, some players are better than others. He is there somewhere. Find him, and work him!

- *Fish out of water:* This player may be pretty skilled, but because of the position he plays he is put in vulnerable situations when adjusting to a spread no-huddle formation. For example:
  - ✓ A *defensive lineman* that must play over an offensive lineman that he doesn't normally line up on
  - ✓ A *linebacker* that is displaced and playing in space rather than a run stopper on the line of scrimmage
  - ✓ A *defensive back* that must guard a man or get to a zone he is not accustomed to
- *A poorly conditioned team:* This is a team that may have a lot of talent, but hasn't put in the time to get in shape. The spread no-huddle attack will challenge this type of team mentally and physically. Poorly conditioned teams normally practice at a slow pace. The tempo of the no-huddle attack will force their brains to fatigue when subjected to the fast pace of the different formations and relentless pace. A poorly conditioned defense will begin to tire and get sloppy with their technique and assignments. You may consider beginning the game against these types of teams with two-minute drill pace coupled with lots of shifts and motions to tax both their mental and physical inferiority.
- *Position group lack of talent:* Some defensive teams are stronger in one area than another. You may look at that week's opponent and see that their front seven has some Hulks that are very good at stopping the run. Don't fret. Spread them out and "play basketball" by sprinting away from their strength and taking the game outside against their weaker defensive backs. If the defense has a strong secondary but a weak line, then "run it down their throat!"

Joseph Fisco/iStock/Thinkstock

"Timing has a lot to do with the outcome of a rain dance."

—Unknown

Marry Run and Pass

Simplify Bootleg and Play-Action: Get 'Em to Bite

Few things are more gratifying for a coach than calling a play-action pass that results in a big play. Whether you're gaining a big first down or setting the defense up for the bomb, the play-action pass is a great way to influence the defense and get a receiver open. When formulating a general game plan versus any opponent, it behooves the offensive coach to insert a play-action passing game that complements the strengths of the run game, not the weaknesses. Don't run play-action passes with run-play paths that are not your better, more productive runs. Defensive players are not fooled by run plays that they aren't worried about. Take advantage of overly aggressive defenses by showing them what they want to see in the run game and taking advantage of their overaggressiveness by getting a receiver open with a play-action pass. Sometimes all you have to do is fool one guy on the defense to gain a strategic advantage that leads to a key first down or, better yet, a touchdown.

Offensive Line Must Do Their Part

It is essential that your offensive line not give away their pass set. They must execute their pass set precisely like the run-action for the first couple small, choppy steps of their takeoff. "Don't show your face; don't show your numbers" is vital for offensive linemen when the defense keys offensive linemen for pass or run. If you can get disciplined defensive players to be unclear about run reads, it might "pop" someone wide open or, at the very least, slow them to their desired location. If, by his uncertainty, you can delay a linebacker for a fraction of a second from getting to his zone or making a tackle, you are working as a team. Don't run a play-action pass unless you have a successful run play to complement it. A play-action passing game must influence a defensive player to overcommit (overreact) to your run stimulus. His overreaction will serve to open up the pass play. Sometimes you might fool the entire defense and have three guys open, or maybe you fool a linebacker just long enough to sneak him open and gain a first down. It might be a matter of gaining one step on a defensive back that allows you to attack deep and "go for six." Whatever your reason to use the play-action pass, you must have a system that is simple, diverse, and effective.

Timing Is of the Essence

Timing of your play-action play call is vitally important. The offensive play caller must be patient and not rush a play-action pass until he has run the run-action and determined that there is a defensive player that is overcommitting and ripe for play-action pass. It is beneficial to have an assistant coach or your eyes in the sky watch your opponent's defense to help you determine who is being overly aggressive in the run game and exploit him. The play caller may not call the play-action pass immediately, but may store the thought into his short-term memory and run it at the next appropriate situation. You must make defenses pay for being overly aggressive. Fool the defense for just a fraction of a second, and you can gain a small yet significant advantage in the pass game. If you are thorough in your scouting, you will notice those defensive backs and linebackers that do not read their line keys and have their eyes focused in the backfield on run plays. These players are very susceptible to play-action pass. Take advantage of unsound, undisciplined, overly aggressive defenders.

Marry Run- and Play-Action

Simplify Terminology

The following is a play-action passing system that is simple yet diverse. It is *simple* in that the offensive line has the exact same blocking scheme for sprint, play-action pass, and bootleg. It is *diverse* because it allows you to run multiple pass plays from multiple formations, utilizing multiple run-actions. It is *effective* because it meets all the down-and-distance as well as situational requirements that come up in a game. Some of you reading this may have a different way of marrying your run- and play-action/bootleg. There are many ways to block bootleg: naked boots, flow boots, waggles, conventional uncovered guard(s) pull, and so forth. If you are having success, *keep doing it*! If you are just implementing the SNH or are looking for another simpler way of seamlessly combining the best of your run- and play-action/bootleg, you might want to consider the following system.

Sprint Pass Blocking

Start with sprint protection. Teach sprint blocking first. Once the player has mastered sprint protection concepts and techniques, he has essentially mastered play-action and bootleg as well. This system of sprint protection is based on run-and-shoot pass protection coached by Mouse Davis. Sprint, play-action, and bootleg are all blocked exactly the same. Designate 50 as sprint left and 60 as sprint right. The odd numbers are all left and even numbers are right. The 5 in 50 is an odd number; therefore, you are sprinting left (Figure 4-1). The 6 in 60 is an even number; thus, you are sprinting right (Figure 4-2). With one sprint-blocking scheme, you add one number to a run-action plus a one-word pass route for an unlimited choice of sprint, boot, and play-action passes.

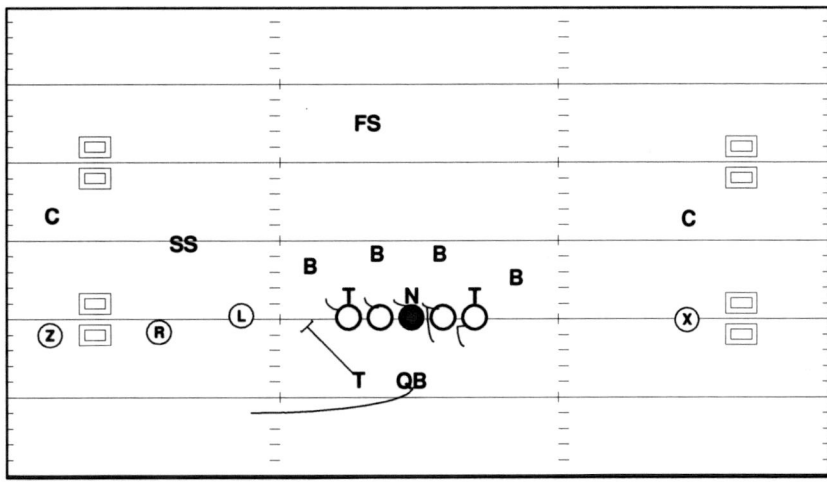

Figure 4-1. 50 pro

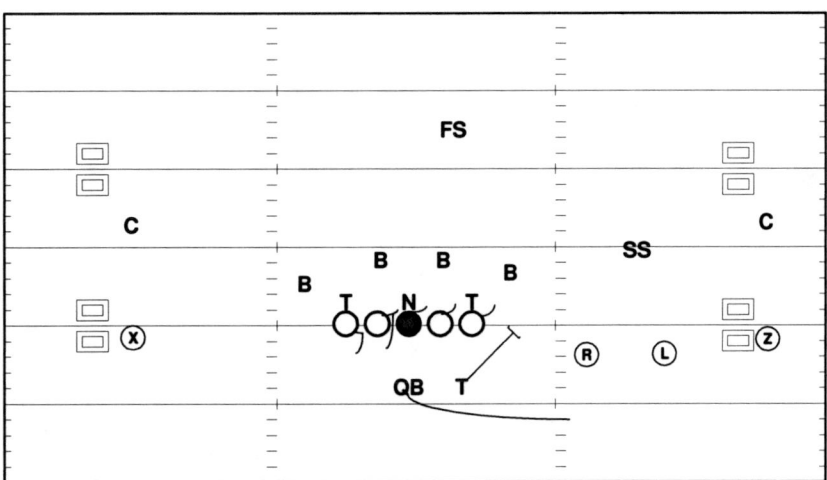

Figure 4-2. 60 pro

Running Back: Starts from the first man outside of the playside tackle. If the first man outside playside tackle rushes, he must collide with him as close to the line of scrimmage as possible, attacking his outside shoulder. If no first man is outside of the playside tackle or he drops into coverage, then the running back works his eyes inside to pick up blitzing linebackers. He works his eyes back, checking for inside linebacker blitz. If no blitz, then he turns completely backside to help the offensive lineman or pick up anyone who has been turned loose.

Offensive Lineman: Blocks big-on-big with defensive lineman nearest to or covering him. If he is uncovered, checks for the linebacker over him. If the linebacker does not come, he turns back (away) from the sprint side, helping his immediate teammate while anticipating the backside rush.

Play-Action Blocking Responsibilities

Putting a 3 before an existing run play tells your back which way to fake and your offensive linemen which way to sprint protect. The 3 tells the offensive linemen to sprint block to the direction of the run-action. If the call is "324," the running back and the quarterback will fake the 24 run play while the 4 (even number) in 324 tells the offensive linemen to block sprint protection to the right. Give a one-word description of the pass play to be run, and you've got a play-action pass. 324 and 60 as well as 325 and 50 are blocked exactly the same in different directions.

Bootleg Blocking Responsibilities

By putting a 2 in front of a run-action, you tell your back which way to fake and your offensive linemen which direction to sprint block. The long "u" sound made when pronouncing *two* tells the offensive line "boot." The 224 call tells the running back and the quarterback to fake 24 run, then the quarterback will bootleg in the opposite direction. The two o's *in bootleg* and *opposite* tell the offensive linemen to sprint protect opposite the run-action. If the play call is 224, then the offensive line will block opposite of the 4 in 224. The numeral 4 is an even number; therefore, the offensive linemen will block 50 or sprint left. Picture the running back and quarterback faking 24 to the right, then the quarterback bootlegging to his left while the offensive linemen block 50 sprint protection. The call 225 tells the running back and quarterback to fake 25 run, then the quarterback will bootleg in the opposite direction. Envision the running back and the quarterback faking 25 to the left, and then the quarterback bootlegging to his right while the offensive linemen block 60 sprint protection. Using the numeral 2 before a run-action tells everyone on the offensive team what play they are faking and what direction requires sprint protection. Add a one-word pass route to the end of the bootleg call, and you have a bootleg play. This very simplified version of bootleg blocking can be very effective. As long as your offensive linemen "don't show their face or numbers" and make it appear as a run. you will maintain solid pass protection while taking advantage of linebackers, strong safeties, and free safeties who are supposed to be keying specific offensive linemen for pass or run, but are eyeing the back rather than their run key.

Figures 4-3 through 4-5 show how you can run the same pass play (stops) from sprint, play-action, and bootleg from the same formation. The offensive line and running backs must know how to block just one protection while the wide receivers memorize one pass play. The combinations are endless. What appears to be an intricate, elaborate, sophisticated passing game to the defense is actually made very simple for the offense to remember and execute.

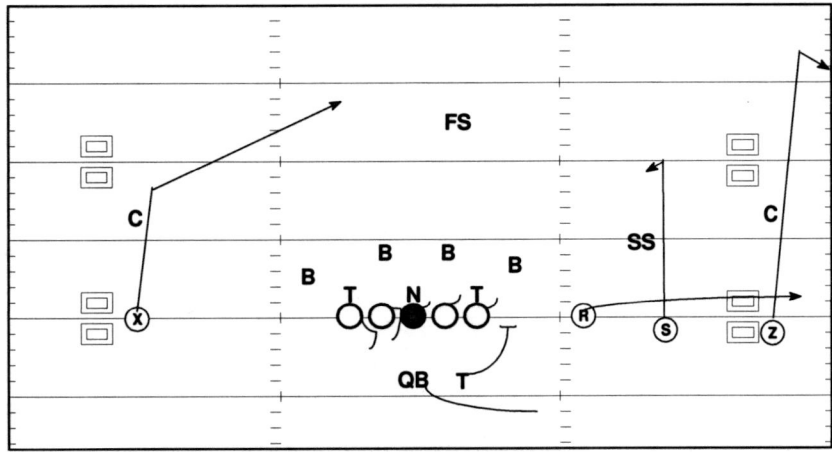

Figure 4-3. Pat 60 stops

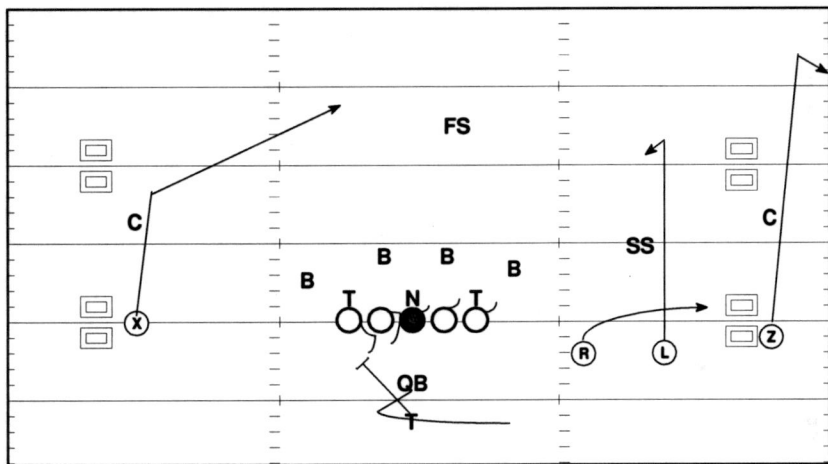

Figure 4-4. Pat 225 stops

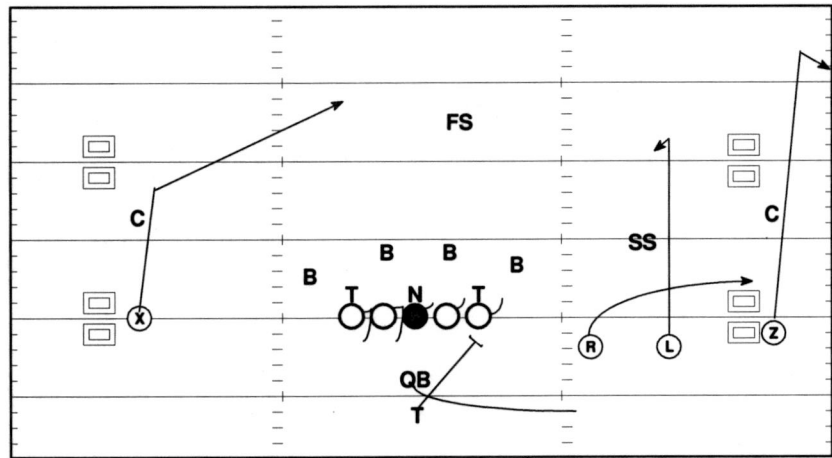

Figure 4-5. Pat 324 stops

"The eight laws of learning
are explanation, demonstration,
imitation, repetition, repetition,
repetition, repetition,
and repetition."

—John Wooden

Simplify Your Communication

Every team has their unique way of communicating their system. A language only to be understood by team members. This language coupled with the signals to communicate it is as important as the plays themselves when it comes to the SNH offense. There are as many ways to communicate terminology as there are teams. What is most important is that your players understand how to quickly receive a signal from a coach and execute the play. Coaches sometimes don't give their players enough credit in memorizing terms and assignments. Players can memorize enough plays and formation calls to run a high-powered offense.

This Isn't the NFL

Have you heard some of the offensive play calls at the professional football level? Mind boggling! The tremendously long play calls you hear NFL quarterbacks make very specifically tells every person what to do on every play. This is not a bad thing, but it does put an extra burden on the quarterback. This makes it easy to plug a new player into the system and not skip a beat. It is also a necessity when it comes to the hundreds, even thousands, of plays that they must memorize over a 16-game season. Every player merely listens to a specific part of the formation and play call and executes his assignment. Keep in mind that NFL players have the luxury of countless hours of meeting and/or practice time every day to learn and digest the vast offensive language that is prevalent in the NFL. Is it any wonder that rookie quarterbacks in the NFL have such a tough time grasping the complexities of a professional offense that has a word, term, or number to describe nearly every player's responsibility on every play?

This kind of communication system is not necessary at the high school level. You don't have the time to meet and present the vast amount of information that the pro's use. You have your players for a limited time every day. Many of you must divide your day or days into offensive and/or defensive emphasis. Your terminology must be concise yet thorough. Most of the teams in the NFL huddle, thus the need for an elaborate signaling system is not necessary. The long play calls in the NFL are done in the huddle by a quarterback that got the play via headset from the coach on the sideline.

Start Communication System on Day One

Introduce your descriptive word routes early in the year, attach signals to them, and repeat them constantly. Repetition is the only way your players will memorize them. The players will learn the meaning of word routes and the corresponding signal amazingly quickly. Much of this has to do with the fact that when the wide receiver hears "flood," he not only remembers his route, but he also gets a feel for everyone else's route around him.

Combine Words and Numbers

> *"Fighting with a large army is no different than fighting with a small one: it is merely a question of instituting signs and signals."*
>
> —Sun Tzu

You want to develop a method of communication that is minimal in words and maximal in meaning. You want a few words to mean a lot and pack a punch. Anytime you can make one word tell numerous players what to do, that is good. This helps in developing a minimum amount of signals that need to be relayed by the sideline coach as well as aiding in the frantic game-time communication that often takes place. These terms are unique to your team. The terms that you and your players come up with will only have meaning to you and your players, nobody else. The terms you use to describe your formations and plays are meaningless to anyone outside of the team. Different coaches call the same things differently, depending on their head coach's set of terms. What words, numbers, or any combination of those you choose to implement is up to you. As long as it is a set of words that describes what you want done and is understandable to your players, then you have a system of communication. Keep in mind that the words you use will have significance to every player in a different way. It is helpful to include your players in the term naming process. Try to have your terminology match the assignment in one way or another. The words you use to describe your plays should have some relationship to each other. Any time you help your players visualize their assignment based on the name of the play it is helpful.

One Word, Multiple Meanings

Implementing an offensive call and signal system that utilizes terms that mean multiple things to multiple players in as few words as possible is optimum. The key to learning this type of system is repetition by the players and discretion by the coach. The coach must also use good discretion in implementing the terms and signals at a pace that is understandable to the players. When and how much should be exposed to the players is key. The right combination of meeting time, walk-throughs, and signal sessions is essential when implementing your communication system in an organized and effective manner. What may appear to be an intricate or elaborate communication system to outsiders will actually be a simple, fast, and efficient mode of communicating between players and coaches. The words used in your offensive system may be funky or off-the-wall, but as long as they have relevance and meaning to every player, it is sufficient. It is interesting to see what names your players will come up with for plays. How and what you and your players devise when it comes to words and the signals used to express those words is up to you. Your system must include signals for formations, shifts, motions, and plays. It can be done. It should be simple yet thorough enough to be able to run any play at any time.

10-Year-Olds Use It

The following ideas will help you simplify your spread no-huddle formation and play calling. This easy-to-learn system works at the youth football level. Yes, the same system used at the high school varsity and college levels has been used very successfully with 10-year-olds. It is also the reason that such an offensive system has been consistently successful year after year regardless of the sometimes-limited mental capacity of players. It can be a savior for a varsity team when JV coaches are unwilling to run the varsity offense and the varsity coach is unable to replace them. You must be able to teach a system to your players that they could grasp in a spring and summer prior to their varsity career and thrive. This system has been years in the making. It started with a desire to minimize the amount of words necessary to specify formations and plays. This system was built to pack the maximum amount of information in a minimum amount of words. Yes, it requires memorization, but, it can be done if you involve your players, keep it simple, teach it in the right progression, and you start the first day of spring practice.

Involve Players in the Play-Calling Process

Amos Alonzo Stagg said, "It is not what the coaches know that counts, but rather what the players have learned." Your players will learn terms and signals faster if you involve them in the brainstorming process. Diagram the play, talk about assignments, walk through responsibilities, and then ask the players what they want to call it. Nine times out of 10, they will come up with a name and signal for the play in less than two minutes of discussion. The name of the play usually bears some resemblance to the play.

Figure 5-1 illustrates a perfect example. It is called *flood*. The players decided to call it "flood" because, as you can see, three wide receivers *flood* an area of the field. Collectively, a signal was devised for the coach to use his hands to illustrate rain coming down from the sky. This is how a play is born, and the players will memorize it faster because they were involved in the process. You will notice that you have three receivers flooding one area of the field. One receiver at depths of short, intermediate, and deep.

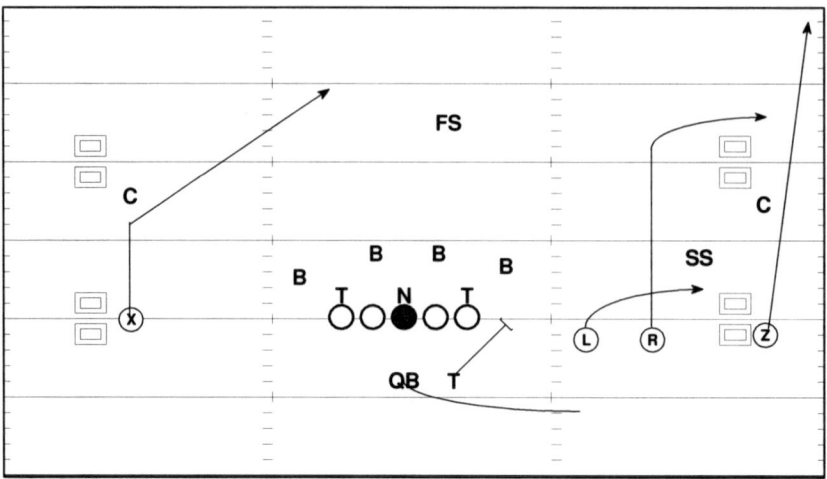

Figure 5-1. Pat 60 flood

One Word, Two Meanings: Naming Formations

I was implementing a spread no-huddle attack at Carmel High School 20 years ago. I wanted to make it very easy to get to trips to the field or double slot after every play. I also wanted to be able to start in double slot and motion to trips to the field fast and efficiently. I needed to develop a quick and easy way to do this. At the time, my wife Patty and I had three small boys: Patrick, Phillip, and Kenneth. I decided to call trips to the right Pat (because of the R in Patrick), trips to the left Phil (because of the L's in Phillip), and Ken was double slot. The players loved it, it was easy to remember, and my kids felt very important. One word Pat and Phil mean line up immediately into trips right or left. The one-syllable words Pat, Phil, and Ken meant go to trips or double slot formation without motioning. To start out in double slot and motion to trips to the field, I would signal in Patrick or Phillip. The full, long name means we motion from Ken to trips (Patrick, Phillip). One word Patrick or Phillip means line up in double slot and motion to trips right or left. Throw a shift in there, and you do a bunch of things with a minimum amount of words. The route and formation possibilities are endless!

You can use any words that work for you. One word designates formation, where to start and where to motion. Throw in the word "shift," and you add an entire new layer.

Play Call Examples

If you signal in the formation Pat or Phil, the players line up immediately into trips right or left. If you signal in Patrick or Phillip, the players start in Ken (double slot), and one man motions to get into trips. If you inject a shift call before a formation, the players will shift from a predesigned formation into Ken (double slot), and then motion into the desired formation. "Shift Patrick" means shifting from one formation into Ken (double slot), then motioning to trips to the right (Patrick). If you want to merely shift into trips without motion, you simply say "Shift Pat" or "Shift Phil." Two words, and you have generated a ton of movement and adjustments for the defense. The great thing about having your offensive terminology simple and minimal is the ability to add deception and/or variances. You can give the defense many different looks and adjustments using a minimum amount of words to describe a large amount of information. Following are some examples of one-word descriptions:

- *Ken* (Figure 5-2): Double slot formation
- *Pat* (Figure 5-3): Trips to the right
- *Phil* (Figure 5-4): Trips to the left
- *Patrick* (Figure 5-5): Starting in Ken and motioning in to trips to the right
- *Phillip* (Figure 5-6): Starting in Ken and motioning in to trips to the left

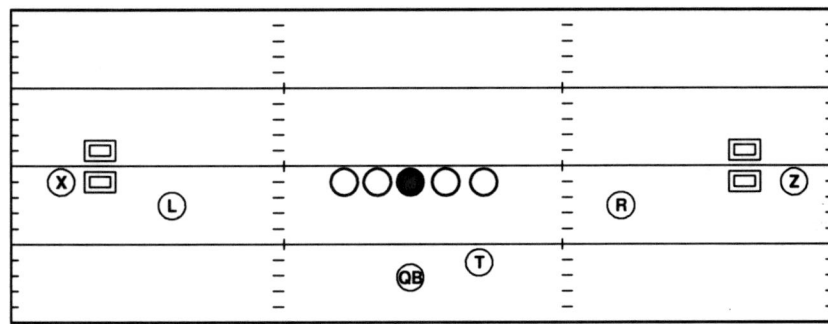

Figure 5-2. Ken formation

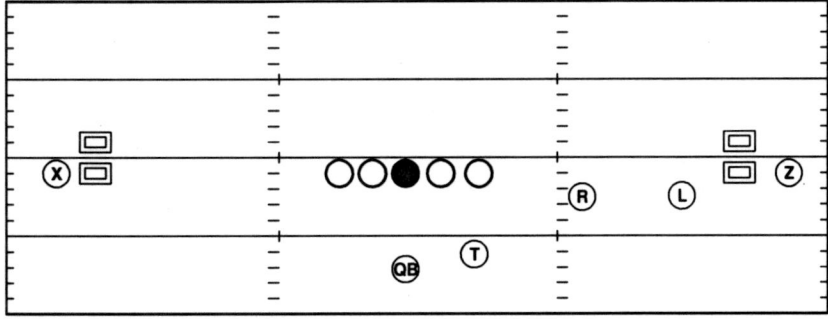

Figure 5-3. Pat formation

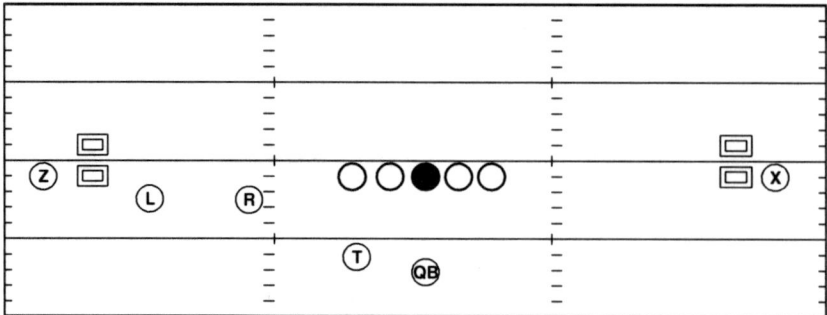

Figure 5-4. Phil formation

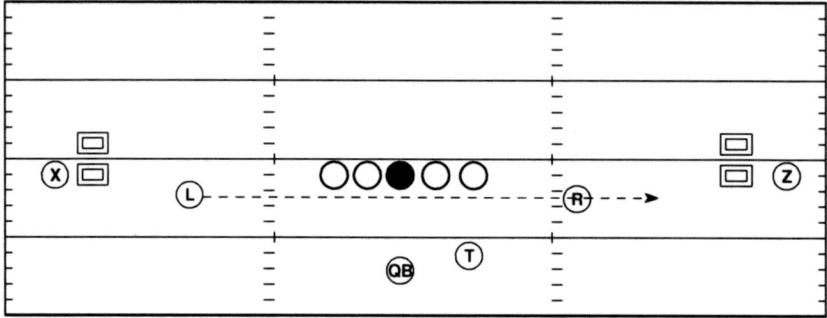

Figure 5-5. Patrick motion

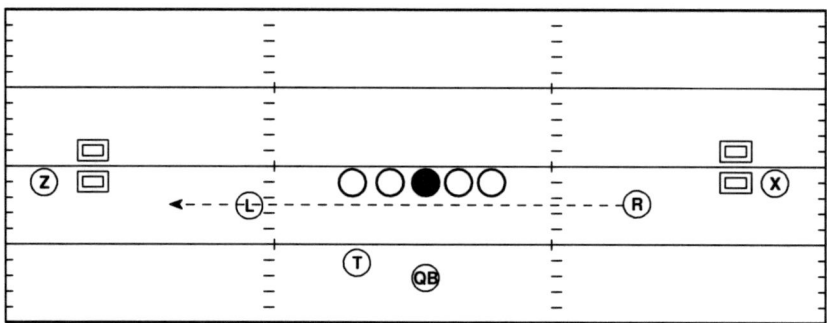

Figure 5-6. Phillip motion

Throw in Tags

Tag means you specify or tag any single receiver's assignment within a word or number route. With a simple numbered passing tree, you can tag any one of the wide receiver routes within a word route. A perfect example would be the play Patrick 60 flood Z 6 (Figure 5-7). Start in Ken, motion to Patrick, everybody runs flood except Z runs a post pattern. If you the coach see that the free safety is overplaying all of those outs, then you may call "60 flood Z 6." This call tells everybody to run 60 flood, but tags the Z to run a 6 route (a post). The quarterback will sprint to his right and eye (look off) the free safety to make him think he is throwing to one of the outs. He then steps up and throws to a wide open Z, who has run a post route into the area the free safety has vacated. Many coaches believe that the single-word system does not allow for flexibility. I disagree. The combination of words, numbers, and tags gives you all the flexibility you need. Look at the adjustments the defense has to make, plus you have the flexibility to tag a route based on a weakness the defense was giving you.

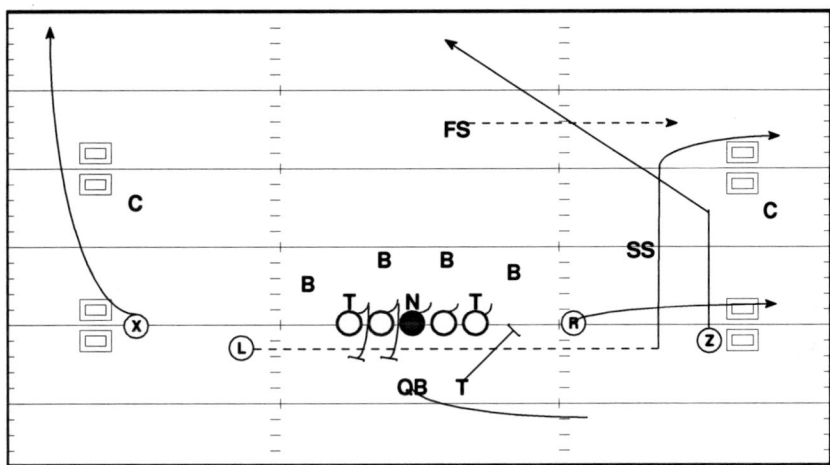

Figure 5-7. Patrick 60 flood Z 6

Communicating the 90 Pass Game

A simple numbering system is all you need for the quick passing game. The call "90 pass" tells the offensive linemen to block 90 technique, which is firing out and blocking aggressively while the quarterback is taking a quick three-step drop. Wide receivers in the 90 pass series mirror their routes, which means they all run the same route called after the 9 in 90. In the case of the play 91, all wide receivers run a 1 route, which is a three-yard out. If you want one of the wide receivers to run a route other than 1, you can tag a specific wide receiver to run a different route. It is very quick and easy to call 90-something and have everybody know what to do while one person does something different. When "91-H2" is called, you are telling all the wide receivers to run 1 routes except wide receiver "H," who runs a 2 route. This is a slant-quick-out combination to trips. You can run any mirrored routes and tag any wide receiver route at any time. The possibilities using this system are endless, especially when you find mismatches in the defensive secondary and tag specific routes to attack weak defenders.

Figure 5-8 is an example of the quick pass 92. The "92" call tells the line how to block, the quarterback how to drop, and the wide receivers what route to run. Notice all of the wide receivers are running the same mirrored routes.

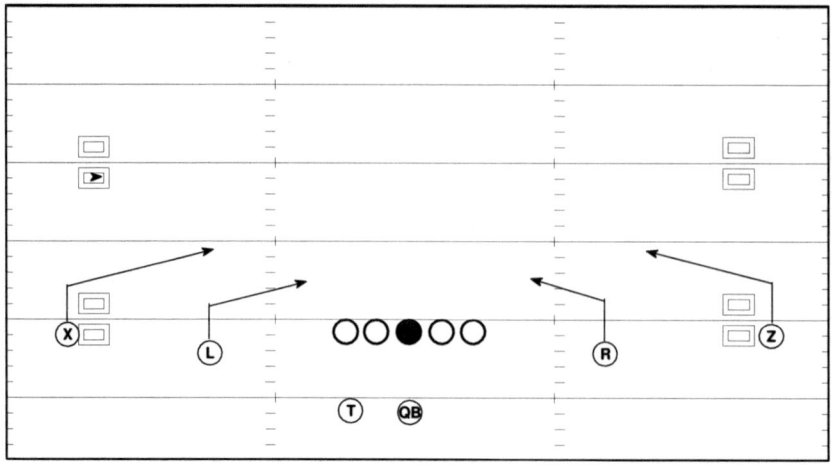

Figure 5-8. 92 pass

Figure 5-9 illustrates mirrored routes by wide receivers with a R tagged to run a 1 route (quick out).

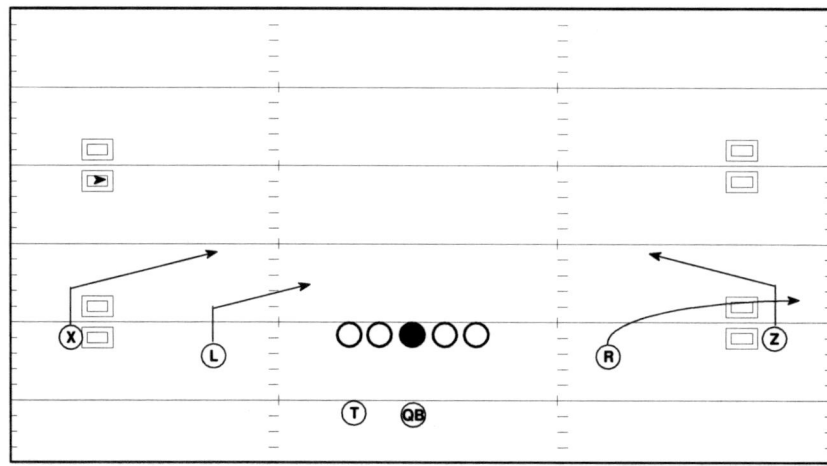

Figure 5-9. 92 R1

The play shown in Figure 5-10 is called 60 trail. The 60 tells the offensive linemen how and in what direction to block, the quarterback how and where to sprint, and the wide receivers to run a trail route.

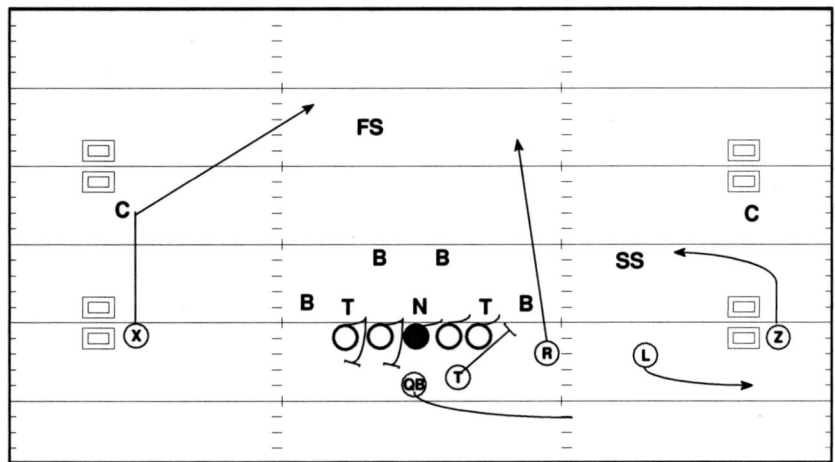

Figure 5-10. Pat 60 trail

"The true test of character is not how much we know how to do, but how we behave when we don't know what to do."

—John Holt

"Get The Edge"

You are the one who is in the absolute best position possible to teach the lessons you want your players to leave your program with. You are the one to model and communicate how and what your players and coaches are going to be. If your only concern is your win-loss record and coach-of-the-year honors, then save yourself some time and put this book down. *Successful* means creating well-rounded citizens, having fun, and winning football games. If you aren't into that, then you will miss out on some of the most fun, intense, and emotional experiences of your life.

A successful football program isn't about going undefeated every year. Anybody that has ever spent time preparing for and participating in a football season knows of the numerous teachable moments that occur on a daily basis. You have all heard how football is like the game of life. Football is not unlike any team endeavor that is attempted by individual human beings. The interaction that takes place between every person involved with your program is a psychology laboratory. Every year, your football team is a unique social experiment. Once you break down the many events that take place between a variety of individuals on a team, it becomes clear that football really is like the game of life. The many types and levels of social interaction you see out in the real world are found on a football team. People are asked to sacrifice personal goals for the good of the company every day in all walks of life. Unlike individual sports, if you play on a team, you will have teammates that you are accountable to just as you are with a workmate in a business or work environment. This accountability to someone else and striving for a common goal is the perfect environment to teach the many lessons your players need to learn as they go down the road of life.

What About Less Glamorous Lessons?

Hard work, perseverance, and teamwork sound really neat and are all great lessons to be learned. They are important lessons that last a lifetime. These three lessons are probably the best sounding and most obvious when referring to lessons learned in football. The lessons that are just as important but discussed less are frustration, humility, defeat, and tolerance. These lessons are not fun. These are the tough lessons. These are the lessons that are just as important as the popular ones, but don't get mentioned because they don't sound as glamorous. Many of the lessons that a young man learns through football are difficult, miserable experiences. Many times, your players will not realize until many years later the lessons they learned from their football experience. At the time they experience them during their playing days, the lessons appear as major obstacles that cause stress, fatigue, and worry. It isn't until years down the road that they look back and realize the lessons learned by overcoming those obstacles. It is up to the coach to anticipate or at least realize those moments that come up through the course of the season and be the adult. Your players will see how you react after a defeat. Your players will be watching the way you respond to every adverse situation that arises. Your physical actions as well as what comes out of your mouth at highly emotional times are the most teachable but difficult moments you will encounter. Model the lessons you want your players to learn. You can rest assured that your players are watching everything you do, all the time.

One of my former players joined the army. He fought in Eastern Europe. During battle, he was forced to become part of the landscape and hide in a field for a couple of days while waiting for help to arrive. He ate insects and all sorts of things to survive. It was a huge media event. When interviewed by a Washington newspaper after the event, he stated, "My high school football coach had this saying that 'Your body can take it; it's the mind that tells you to quit.' I just kept telling myself 'My body can take it,' and it did." When that newspaperman called me and told me what had happened, it was one of the proudest moments of my life. I didn't think anyone was listening. I made a difference!

Those of us who have been around awhile can tell stories about former players that come back years later and recite verbatim entire speeches or comments that you made. Your players remember how you reacted to specific events, what you said, and how it made them feel. I hope you, reading this book, understand how influential you are to your players. For some players, you may be the only male, fatherly figure they have in their life. If they don't learn some of these lessons from you, they may never learn them. Embrace this opportunity to make a difference in a young man's life.

Team Above Self

Pat Riley, the great basketball coach has a saying: "Commitment to the team—there is no such thing as in-between, you are either in or out." One of the beautiful things about team sports is: to work for something bigger than yourself. To learn that feeling of working with and counting on your teammate to do his job while you do your job is an invaluable lesson that can last a lifetime. For many players, this might be the last time they are actually on an athletic team. Hopefully, you have instilled in them the sense of purpose and teamwork necessary to function on a non-athletic team. Have you noticed how many companies in the business world call their workforce a "team?" They use this term because it takes a cohesive team to generate a profit. It takes every individual sacrificing his own personal goals for the sake of the group.

Some individuals, players, and coaches won't get this at first. It is hard for some players to understand what matters most is team success, not personal achievement. Some players are so wrapped up in their own statistics and glory they are unable to see the big picture. They are only happy when they get their name in the paper. This should come as no surprise to the coach. Not every player will embrace the "one for all and all for one" attitude. This attitude may be fueled by parents who live vicariously through their son and expose him to constant attention to stats and other interests that do not serve the betterment of the team. This attitude must be modified before individual pursuits override team goals. "Play for the name on the front of the jersey, not the back."

Learn Respect

Players must learn to respect the many different personalities that can be present on a football team. Not every player will be friends with every teammate, but a sense of trust and respect should transcend any differences they may have. Teammates may not like each other, but they must respect each other. Some guys will just not get along with other guys. That doesn't mean they can't function together in a team environment. It certainly doesn't mean that they are enemies or can't put the team ahead of their differences. The only way to truly get this done is if every player has a certain amount of respect for himself. It is extremely difficult to exert the energy necessary to understand and empathize with a teammate if at first you don't respect yourself as an individual. There is no better environment to facilitate mutual respect than a team setting. A vast array of beliefs and/or ethnicities can be present on a single team. Tolerance and empathy for each other is crucial, not being best buddies. It is up to the head coach to recognize intolerance and stomp it out immediately. Bigotry and intolerance can tear a team apart. If not addressed immediately, and left to fester, issues of disrespect between players can turn a good team into a bad team. The coach can facilitate this attitude of appreciating differences by publicly recognizing the individuality of each player. Foster a sense of celebrating differences rather than hanging on to old beliefs.

Your team may be a melting pot. You may have reds playing with blues. As long as you can get everyone playing for the color of the jersey, you will be okay. This goes back to a theory previously discussed that once teammates experience discomfort or pain together, they bond. Miraculous diplomatic events occur every day on the football field. Various belief systems and cultural baggage get thrown aside in favor of competing as a team. Young men disregard what the newspapers say about society and fight alongside each other on the field regardless of their race, creed, or color. The coach must establish an environment that fosters unity and respect for every individual on the team. It could be the most important lesson they take with them.

You don't have to treat everyone exactly the same, but you must be fair. You must be consistent, not ambivalent about how you allow your players to speak to each other. Teenagers have their own language. That being said, certain lines cannot be crossed. Words cut sharper than knives. You cannot let fun social banter become a hurtful experience to an innocent player. Kids can be ruthless and not be aware of it. Some players are not taught tolerance and/or acceptance at home. It is up to you to foster a climate of acceptance and accountability where everyone is valued for their contribution to the team, not the color of their skin or what God they believe in.

Learn Empathy

A team is made up of many different individuals. Different races, religions, socioeconomic status, and cultural influences are prevalent on many teams. The team experience they are having with you could be the first and only time some of these players have been exposed to cultural diversity. Your time on the field may be the only two hours of the day that some of your players will spend together. Many of your players will depart the locker room and go to vastly different environments.

This successful football experience is a perfect time for players to become aware of the differences in people, but also the similarities. Spending countless hours together in preparation for and participating on a football team can be the glue that binds the different belief systems that exist on a team. "We all wear the same color jersey." Developing an understanding and sense of empathy for a teammate who is different is a lesson more valuable than winning football games.

My first year of college football was spent living in the jock dorm. After about the third night of camp, I felt it necessary to approach my next-door neighbor and ask him to turn the volume of his stereo down. It was the third night in a row that loud music had emanated from his room until the wee hours. I was aware that my neighbor was African-American, but I didn't care about that; I just wanted him to turn his stereo down a bit. When I knocked on his door, he opened it about five inches. I could see just half of his head. He asked, "What's up?" so I told him I would appreciate if he could turn the volume down. He said "Sure" and closed the door. He turned his stereo down, and everything was cool.

Something about that brief experience didn't feel right. Over the course of the next few days, I noticed he had a hankering for Schlitz malt liquor. I wanted him to know there were no hard feelings, so one night I knocked on his door with a six-pack of Schlitz talls. Again, he only opened the door about five inches. I asked him if I could come in. He saw that I was bearing gifts, so he reluctantly complied. That was the start of a whole new world for the both of us.

Time does not allow me to list all the topics we discussed that night, but what I will say is our conversation lasted until the sun came up. At the end of the conversation, he told me that the only time he had ever spoken to a white person, other than me, was his recruiting coach. He certainly never had a social conversation with a white person before. He had lived in the deep inner city of Los Angeles his entire life and had never had an occasion to speak to a white person, let alone have a conversation. We bent each other's ears all night. He told me what experiences contributed to his beliefs, and I shared mine. To this day, I can't tell you whether he felt comfortable with me or if it was the Schlitz that got him talking. I don't care! We both learned empathy that night. He discovered that I didn't fit the stereotype that he had of me, and I learned to better appreciate where he was coming from—figuratively and literally. I left his room with a much deeper knowledge and appreciation for his point of view and he of mine. We discovered that we had much more in common than we had differences. I got a feel for how it was to walk in his shoes and vice versa. Without a team setting, both of us might never have had that life-changing conversation. It was very gratifying for me to watch him blossom socially over the next four years. He developed lifelong friendships with teammates of every ethnicity.

Try Hard When the Chips Are Down

Your true character will shine for all to see when the chips are down. Every team, good or bad, will experience difficult situations throughout a football season. How you react to and deal with these difficult situations will be the difference between success and failure. It is up to the coach to be the example when facing the many bumps in the road that occur over the course of a season. It is easy to be the example when all is going well, but it is going to be your leadership during strife and adversity that is going to be the best lesson they could ever learn. It is how you react to adversity that will be the best lesson for your players. Losing a game(s), being behind at halftime, incurring a crucial penalty, and so forth are all teachable moments that require the coach to model the behavior he would like from his players.

A few years back we lost a game by a large margin. On the Monday following the game, the coaches decided to have a rare team meeting. I have never been a fan of team gripe sessions, but sometimes it is absolutely imperative that the entire team meet to clarify issues that come up or clear the air. My point to the team was that I felt like they did not play hard when they got down. I felt as though they quit before the game was over.

After I vented, I gave the players a chance to talk. What happened next has stayed with me to this day. One of our leaders stood up and said, "We aren't the only ones who quit, Coach. You quit on us!" You could have heard a pin drop. "I don't understand," I said. "I coached you guys to the bitter end." He said, "You took your headset off halfway through the fourth quarter. You stopped coaching us. Everybody saw you take your headset off and put it on the bench." He was right. I did take my headset off. He was wrong that I quit coaching, but that didn't matter. That is what the players saw, so that is what they believed. They saw me take my headset off, period. Any coaching I did after that was ignored because they were not only embarrassed about their performance, they were disappointed in me for giving up on them. They saw my actions as quitting and that is the most important thing. They merely followed my example. What was innocent behavior on my part was viewed by the players as not caring or raising the white flag. In my mind, I took the headset off because I deemed it unnecessary. We were going to keep the ball on the ground, chew up some clock, and get the hell out of there. They viewed my actions much differently. I apologized and told them that would never happen again, and it hasn't.

What a wonderful lesson I learned that day. I realized that my players are watching every move I make on the sideline, *especially* when the going is tough or the chips are down. I should not expect anything out of my players that I don't model myself. In my mind, I did not quit, but in the players' minds I did. I learned the hard way that I can't expect anything out of my players that I am not an example of. I assure you that, from that day on, I have never taken my headset off before the game is over. Whether we are winning or losing, as weird as it sounds, I know that, in that one instance, the players perceived my effort by whether I kept my headset on the entire game. I'm glad I did not get defensive when reprimanded by my player. It enabled me to learn a very valuable lesson, and in turn my players appreciated the fact that I heard what they had to say. We came together, won the conference, and went to a bowl game.

Great Accomplishments Require Hard Work

"Industriousness is the most conscientious, assiduous, and inspired type of work. A willingness to, an appetite for, hard work must be present for success. Without it, you have nothing to build on."

—John Wooden

Those of us who have been lucky enough to be involved with the game of football know the amount of time and effort it takes to be successful. Between off-season conditioning, spring practice, summer conditioning, fall camp, a long season, and playoffs, it is a grind. Academic and extracurricular activities also take a bite out of the football players' time. Preparing for and participating in a high-powered football program involves a great deal of hard work.

Value Humor

When I first took over the program at Carmel High School I was dead set on showing everyone how serious I was about turning the program around. I was going to show everyone what a no-nonsense, intense coach looks like. I felt like if I showed any light-heartedness or humor, it would be construed as soft or lackadaisical. I did this for a full year or so until a trusted assistant approached me and wanted to have a serious talk.

In simple terms, he told me to lighten up. "You walk around here with a snarl on your face all the time. You look like you've got a perpetual stick up your ass. Loosen up, show the players that sense of humor I know you have. You have the entire team walking on eggshells at all times because you constantly exude this serious life-or-death attitude about everything. I think you, the players, and coaches will have more fun and be more productive if you smile once in a while. The players know how serious you are and how much you care. It is not necessary to be so uptight all the time. Look like you are having fun every now and then. You may be surprised with the results."

Wow. What an eye-opener that was. I hope some of you are as lucky as I was to have an assistant who feels comfortable enough to be brutally honest with you. I followed his advice, and it made a world of difference. It was a win-win. I had a huge weight taken off my shoulders, and the players enjoyed their time around me more. I no longer felt the need to show everyone how much I cared about the program. The players could tell by my work ethic. I didn't need the snarl to prove I could get the job done. The players saw a whole different side of me. They began to see me as a human being rather than a monster. I didn't change my personality. I merely exposed the players to a side of my personality that existed the whole time, but I hadn't showed. It wasn't like I became a stand-up comic. I just put a smile on my face and acted like I was enjoying myself, which I was. I showed the players that I was capable of smiling, even laughing! This was all done within my own personality. I didn't alter the way I was. My assistant was right. The results were amazing. I pick my time and place to interject humor into the process, and the players appreciate that. We got more done and had more fun doing it. Let the players see your lighter side. Show them your sense of humor.

Let Players Show Their Sense of Humor

Let your players express their humor as well. Don't stifle their ability to be funny; enjoy it. Some of your players are hilarious if you let them be. Don't make players feel uncomfortable for cracking a joke or giving some good-humored ribbing to a teammate once in a while. Players and coaches spend a great deal of time together. Much of that time is devoted to serious, hard work, but you can't be serious all the time. You must allow for some levity and humor from your players, or you run the risk of having a team but no fun.

You will find that some of your players are extremely witty and good-natured. They will come to know your limitations as to when and how much humor should be used as they get to know you. Most of them get pretty good at picking their time and place to show you their funny side. You may have to develop a familiar catch phrase that brings the players back to the task at hand once a bit of humor has been thrown into the situation. Comments such as "Good joke, Ralphie! Now let's get back to work" or "That's a good one, Omeed. Now, where were we?" are phrases you can use to bring the group back to attention.

Anticipate, Cooperate, Delegate

There is a chain of command in successful organizations. There are three roles that are most prevalent in a work environment or team. Each role requires specific action, or productivity will break down.

- *Anticipate: When you are a subordinate, you must anticipate what your superior wants.* Players anticipate what their coaches want, assistant coaches anticipate what the head coach wants, head coaches anticipate what their athletic director or principal wants. When this chain of command is followed and respected, everyone wins. Subordinates need not spend time concerning themselves with matters that do not pertain to them. They are to perform their task anticipating what their superior wants and not waste valuable time evaluating decisions that are not theirs to make.

- *Cooperate: When you are equal to a co-worker, cooperate.* When working together side-by-side, cooperation and respect are important. Don't confuse getting along with cooperation. Colleagues or teammates don't have to like each other, but they must cooperate. They may not get along, but it doesn't mean they can't continue to function as a team. Individual differences must be set aside for the good of the cause at some point, or the process of winning comes to a halt. Maybe not immediately, but over time strife, ill feelings, and disharmony can ruin a football team. Getting everyone cooperating at the same time can be done. If problems are addressed swiftly and consistently, everyone within the organization will understand what the expectations are and abide by them. Everyone is different, but some semblance of harmony must prevail. Help your players learn how to cooperate by teaching them. Conduct an intense drill between two position groups, and then require the players to give each other a high-five immediately afterward. Settle any disputes with that high-five. Don't assume your players know how to settle differences and cooperate. Teach them.

  Cooperation also pertains to the many off the field experiences your players may have on behalf of the team. When your player volunteers in the name of your team to load boxes for a charity, staff a marathon, fund-raise outside a market, serve food at a shelter, or such, he learns to cooperate with persons other than the team. Get your team involved with community projects. The team will be viewed as a positive force in the community, and your players will get a crash course in cooperation.

- *Delegate: When in charge, delegate.* The people you choose to surround yourself with are crucial. They will be your face and voice on the field and in public. Vince Lombardi once said, "The strength of the group is the strength of the leaders." The delegation of responsibility involves every person that will be involved with your program. From every coach in the program to the frosh equipment manager, it is up to you to place the right people in the right positions to make it thrive. A leader will have a sense of who should be where. There is no better feeling for a varsity head coach to look over to the freshman practice field and watch them running the same plays, emphasizing the same teaching points, and exhibiting the same enthusiasm as your team. This happens when the head coach delegates responsibility to coaches that have the best interest of the program in mind and are willing to subjugate their personal beliefs and desires and teach what the program teaches and not what worked for them in high school. You are the head coach. Choose loyalty over knowledge. You want to give your assistants their autonomy, but it must exercised within the constraints of the program. An assistant who is loyal, a good teacher, and willing to learn is worth his weight in gold. They will do what you want them to do, not second-guess every decision you make, and have a fun, self-fulfilling experience. Eliminate those assistants who are not loyal or don't believe in your cause. You may have had good intentions when initially hiring an assistant, but sometimes things just don't work out. Be diplomatic, but be swift. The sooner this element is removed from your program, the better.

"Beat 'em to the punch!"

—Bill Walsh

Change the Snap Count

It's amazing how many offensive coaches do not adhere to the simple concept of changing the snap count. Are they lazy or just naive to the fact that, if you don't mix up the snap count, the defense will gain an advantage?

The first thing a good defensive coordinator wants to know when scouting an opposing offense is: "What is the offense's snap count?" As a defensive coordinator, if you can predict when the ball will be hiked on every play, you gain an advantage. What good is it to diagram blocking schemes assuming that your blocker will be able to overtake the person in front of him, yet you put him at a disadvantage by hiking the ball on the same count every time, making it much more difficult for him to gain any head, feet, or hand priority on the block?

To win championships, to defeat teams whose front seven are equal to and/or physically superior to your front seven, you need to gain every advantage you can. An offense can gain advantages in the pass or run game by simply mixing up the snap count. When you give your offensive lineman the half-step advantage on either a run or pass play, you make it easier for him to execute his assignment. As Bill Walsh would say, "Beat 'em to the punch." When an offensive lineman can gain an advantage by merely getting a jump on his defensive opponent, he has a better chance of executing his block successfully. You're giving your opponent an advantage when he consistently knows when to fire out and create havoc within your offensive blocking scheme.

Many elaborate cadences take place at the pro and college levels. Professional and collegiate teams have a great deal more time to implement and practice more complex cadences. Silent counts, dummy calls, anticipatory takeoffs, and such are certainly the more sophisticated techniques used by the pros and major colleges.

A Simple Yet Effective Cadence

Even with a cadence as simple as down-set-hike, you have three ways or three different times you can take off on the football. Many coaches have their quarterback go through an elaborate cadence at the line of scrimmage, but hike the ball on the same count every time. By simply using the cadence "down-set-hike" but hiking the ball at three different times, you gain more of an advantage then if you were to use an elaborate snap count or cadence and still hike it on the same count. If your cadence is "down-color-number-color-number-set-hike-hike" and you snap the ball on the first hike every time, you don't fool anybody. The defense will soon have a half-step advantage over your blockers because they take off on exactly the same count every time.

Six Ways to Change the Snap Count

The following cadence gives you six different snap possibilities: "Down-color-number-color-number-set-hike-hike." The quarterback comes up to the line and says "Down" to get his team ready or get them in to the stance you want them to be in. He then says "Blue-30-blue-30-set-hike-hike" or any color or number that is not considered hot. Theoretically, the ball could be snapped on the first syllable of any of those words or numbers. If you have a quarterback that has the ability to change plays on the line of scrimmage, then you will have a hot color that tells the offensive team that the number called after the hot color is the new play. Have your quarterback say "Easy, easy" if the snap count was originally going to be on the first or second color so he is able to execute his audible call and change the play. Once he calls an audible, the snap count is automatically on one.

The quarterback lets the team know when the ball will be hiked by telling them the snap count is either on sound, meaning the ball will be snapped on the first syllable in *down*, or on "first," meaning the ball will be hiked on the first syllable of the first color, or on "second," meaning the ball will be hiked on the first syllable of the second color. Set if it is set. If the count is on "one" or "two," then the ball will be hiked on the first hike or second hike. This illustrates how to change your snap count six ways. This approach is more than enough to keep the defense off balance.

Train your players to anticipate what the snap count is and take off on the first syllable of the count. By changing the snap count six ways and having your linemen take off on the first syllable of the count, you help your linemen gain at least a half-step advantage on their opponent.

Implement Varying Snap Count on Day One

Your quarterback must be disciplined in the heat of battle to keep changing the count, and your linemen must be disciplined enough to pay attention to the snap count on every play. In order for this to occur, you must begin this process the first day of spring practice and incorporate it into every drill all year round. Linemen and running backs are the only players who need to know the snap count. Wide receivers will be out wide in their formation, getting their splits and finding their landmarks. They do not know what the snap count is. They look inside and take off when they see that the ball is hiked.

"In battle there are not more than two methods of attack—the direct and the indirect, yet these two in combination give rise to an endless series of maneuvers."

—Sun Tzu

Mix Speed and Tempo

Running a no-huddle offense does not mean that you are going 100 miles per hour all the time. While you may have times when you want to go at a very fast tempo, you may also have times that, for various reasons, you want to slow it down a little or slow it down a lot. If you are a defensive coach, I don't need to tell you what kind of anxiety it causes facing a spread no-huddle offense. You must not only be prepared for the various formations, motions, and plays that the offensive team may throw at you that week, but you also know that you must have your defensive signals ready faster than you would against a team that huddles. Maybe you have seen the SNH team you are facing mix up the pace of their attack, fluctuating throughout the game between a fast and slow pace. If this is the case, then it may be necessary to scale down your defensive adjustments and alignments in order to make sure that your defensive team will be able to line up properly and swiftly to a wide variety of formations as well as adjusting to an offense that could be in two-minute mode at any time. The speed and tempo with which you employ the SNH offense can be as important as the actual plays you run. You may go an entire game in the same speed or you may vary the speeds constantly. It is up to you to choose what speed(s) are most appropriate for the opponent you are facing. Changing the rate at which your plays are run serves to make the plays you run more effective.

Change Tempo for a Purpose

Your choice of tempo should have a purpose. Go too fast too much, and you run the risk of tiring your guys out or immediately giving your opponent the ball back. Go too slow, and you let an inferior team hang on when you could speed up the tempo and blow them out. It is up to the coach to use his own good discretion to decide when to speed it up or slow it down.

An offensive coach should have more than enough ways to cause defensive anxiety between tempo, shifting, motioning, and the full gamut of offensive plays. This section will discuss very specific reasons for your choice of tempo. Your decision must weigh the various game and personnel circumstances that may arise. As those who run the SNH offense would say, "Defensive coaches may get into vanilla coverage in order to defend all the looks you may get as well as adapt to the various speeds he may encounter." His defensive substitution plan may have to change if he is facing an SNH team that constantly changes tempo. At any time, you can change to fast tempo and either snap the ball before substitutions are made or snap the ball before he can get his subs on or off the field. These little things drive defensive coaches nuts.

Speeds to Your No-Huddle

Mix up your tempo with three distinct speeds. The no-huddle has three speeds, and it is up to you to decide how and/or when to employ them. You can identify your speeds by color, so as a coach all you have to do is communicate a one-word color to the players on the field, and they know the speed at which to operate.

Green

Green is a fast, hurry-up, two-minute drill tempo. 100 mph. You are operating at full two-minute drill speed. Everything is accelerated. Stay in one formation so the players can get from one play to the next faster. You can get into other formations, but staying in one formation allows for a minimum of adjusting between players.

Use the fast tempo speed at any time during the game. Occasionally, start a game in green mode. Sometimes, based on the opponent, it is important to set the tempo right out of the blocks. By starting the game in green tempo, you are telling your opponent they better have their defensive act together or you are going to operate at 100 mph speed until they do. It is a great confidence-booster for your team if you can take control of the game on your first series or unexpectedly in the middle of the game. This speed, when used as a surprise, creates a great deal of anxiety and/or confusion to the defensive team, not to mention compromises their defensive calls or substitution plan. It is very typical for the defense to remain in one defensive alignment while you are in green mode because you have taken away their ability to communicate defensive adjustments, substitutions, or disguises. Obviously, you can't remain in green mode the entire game but using it as a tool to catch your opponent off-guard at the beginning or middle of the game is useful and fun.

You can easily employ this speed at the beginning, middle, or end of the game when the two-minute drill is necessary. You can operate smoothly in green mode if you do it daily as part of your conditioning. By practicing it as conditioning, it becomes second nature to the players. They operate the two-minute drill with much more confidence in game situations. That's exactly what you want: your players playing confident and fresh at the end of a game when you must score.

Yellow

Yellow is regular speed that allows the offensive team to transition from one play to the next in about the same time as if they were huddling. Because of your no-huddle, the defense is unable to huddle and must get lined up or run the risk of the ball being snapped when they are not ready. Although this speed is executed at normal tempo, the defense must still eliminate its huddle and get lined up in approximately the formation that they will be in at the snap of the ball. Regardless of what tempo you are in, you are not huddling! The defense must respect the fact that you could snap the ball at any time. This is why you will see most defensive strategy changes between series or time-outs and rarely between plays.

Yellow is a great tempo to use when you, as a coach, want to get a good look at what defense your opponent is in before you call a play. Normally, you have plenty of time after the ball is whistled into play to get your team into a formation and see what the defense has in mind. This is time when a team that huddles is making their way back to the huddle, waiting for the play, breaking the huddle, and getting to the line of scrimmage.

You can see that the no-huddle at regular tempo not only gives you a chance to see what formation the defense is in, it also gives you a few more seconds to think about your play call. The extra time that you gain by not huddling gives you more time to shift, motion, and shift/motion if you choose. These things require time—time you don't have when you huddle. At times, you can leave your offense standing out in formation for what seems like an eternity. By not having to run all the way back to the huddle, it gives the offense time to catch their breath, get lined up, and look for the signals from the sideline. Obviously, if the next play you want to run entails a shift, motion, or shift/motion, you must get the play in a little sooner, but if it doesn't this allows you the luxury of taking your time to select your play. You could be using your freeze strategy on offense where you begin your cadence and motion to see how the defense plans on adjusting then freeze, line up in the perfect formation for what the defense has shown, and run a suitable play. You may shift your formation, then freeze, look over to the coach and receive a play.

Red

Red is a slow, milk-it tempo When in red tempo, assign a coach to have a stopwatch that he starts when the referee blows the ready-for-play whistle. This coach notifies the coach who gives the signals when six seconds remain to snap the ball. The coach gives a quick signal to the quarterback that he can snap the ball, and the quarterback goes through a very abbreviated cadence, hiking the ball with one to two seconds left on the 25-second clock. Take as much time off the clock as possible. You could have various reasons for such a slow tempo. Maybe you want to slow the tempo down because you possess a lead and want to milk the clock. Maybe the opposition has an explosive offense, and you don't want them to have the ball. This approach takes time, and you have it in red tempo.

The Game's Not Over!

The game is not over in red tempo. Keep getting first downs until victory formation. The most important concept you must pass on to your players is that the game is not over when you go into red tempo. You are not running the clock out to kneel on the ball. You take a knee when the game is in hand and you are in victory formation only. You must be explosive when executing the play, even though the tempo between the plays is not going 100 mph. You need productive plays that get first downs or scores. You are not sitting on the ball; you are merely using as much time as possible between plays. Sometimes players unconsciously reduce their effort because they mistakenly believe that the game is in hand. That may be true, but you may also need first downs to eat up the clock and secure victory. Remind your players that once the ball is snapped in red tempo, they go 100 percent until they are kneeling on the ball.

"The greatest of all faults is to be conscious of none."

—Thomas Carlyle, English author

Scout Yourself as Well as Your Opponent

Many offensive coaches spend endless hours scouting and researching their opponent's defense. How many of you spend an equal amount of time scouting yourself? If you are an offensive coach working in the same office as your defensive coordinator, you can see what type of tendencies he is trying to glean from watching the opposing team's offense. You must assume the team you will be playing on Friday night will be analyzing the following:

- What plays you run from specific formations
- Your ratio of run to pass in general
- Your ratio of run to pass in specific formations
- Your ratio of run to pass from different spots on the field
- Your favorite formations
- Your favorite plays from those formations
- Your favorite plays based on down-and-distance
- Your favorite plays based on your field position
- Your favorite players that get the ball based on down-and-distance, formation and/or position on the field, or crucial situation
- Specific plays you run with various motions
- What plays you run in crucial, pressure situations
- Your players' strengths, weaknesses, and abilities
- Your coaching strengths, weaknesses, and abilities
- Your cadence
- Stance and alignment keys that give away the play you are going to run
- Your signals

- Your favorite two-point play
- Your favorite third and fourth down short-yardage plays

These tendencies are just of the few criteria used when self-scouting. It is important to be aware of what your tendencies are, but also keep in mind that until you get a few games under your belt and face a variety of defenses, your stats may not be completely reliable. Every game you play is inherently different from the next; therefore, the more input you have, the better. Throughout the course of a season, you will have games, based on what the defense is giving you, that you will emphasize run or pass more than another. This is normal, but over time it is wise to take a good look at how you are attacking opponents that run similar defensive schemes. Your plan of attack can change from year to year or game to game, depending on all the factors that play into what you are going to do offensively to your next opponent.

Sorry, You're Human

Whether you want to believe so or not, you become predictable over time. After all, you're only human. You have your favorite plays for nearly every down-and-distance, formation, and/or place on the field. Even when you believe within yourself that you break tendencies in all of these situations, if you take a closer look you will quickly realize that you become predictable. Some coaches are worse than others. They run the same plays from the same formations from the same position on the field every game. If your team is physically superior to your opponents, then it really doesn't matter if they know what you are doing before you do it. This situation is rare. Only through thorough circumspection and detailed analysis can you honestly determine what your actual tendencies are. Stats don't lie. This information may not sway you a bit if you have been enjoying offensive success, but if you haven't then your analysis may be a much-needed wake up call. You may realize how and why the defensive coordinator on the other side of the field is shouting out what play you are going to run before you run it.

> *"If you know the enemy and know yourself, you need not fear the result of a hundred battles."*
>
> —Sun Tzu

Playing to Your Strength vs. Being Predictable

There is a fine line between playing to your strengths and becoming predictable. As a coach, you will surely be tempted to get your stronger, more reliable players involved in crucial situations. Example: if it's fourth-and-one with the game on the line, your inclination may be to get your best back the ball running behind your best lineman. When it's crunch time, you have a tendency to revert back to plays that have been successful for you in the past. You are so confident that your best players will make the play work, you ignore the fact that your opponent knows where you are going and who is going to get the ball. The play may still work, but you have made the situation more difficult for yourself and run the risk of not converting the fourth down by possibly exposing your team to a play that is impossible to execute because your opponent will end up having more players at the point of attack than your team has blockers. In this situation, your best lineman may make his block, but there may be two extra defenders who are not blocked that make the play. Your intent is good, but your method is flawed.

Scout Yourself to Anticipate Defense

By scouting yourself, you can have the best of both worlds. You can get the ball to your best back running behind your best lineman, but disguise it in such a way that your opponent doesn't know where you are going or at least is balanced up, giving you a chance to not be outmanned. By scouting yourself and knowing that the last five times on fourth-and-one you ran a specific run play, you can now run a play-action that causes the defense to overreact to the run and get a receiver open. If your team is physically talented enough to run a successful play even if the defense knows what's coming, then by all means run the play. Some teams may not be able to do this; therefore, it is wise to scout yourself and break tendencies when possible.

Many scouting programs are available. Examine what ways you have become predictable and break those tendencies. Only by scouting yourself statistically can you truly discern what you do and when. This is not to suggest that you analyze yourself to the point where you are reluctant to play to your strengths. You must. The suggestion is to examine whether you have other ways to play to your strengths without becoming predictable.

"If you're killin' time, it is not murder; it is suicide."

—Lou Holtz

Have a Sense of Urgency

You Can Feel the Tempo

Definition of tempo: rate, rhythm, or pattern of activity. Have you ever experienced, felt, the tempo of a successful team (high school, college, or professional) while they get things done? It oozes from everyone, from players to coaches to support personnel. Their posture, attitude, language, and demeanor exude excellence, confidence, purpose, and a sense of urgency (SOU). Within a successful team/organization, an SOU and singleness of purpose is evident in *every* activity—from training sessions, to practice, warm-ups, meetings, film sessions, walk-throughs, rehab, and pre-game meals. SOU doesn't mean every activity is done at breakneck speed or a frenetic pace. It certainly doesn't mean you do things fast just for the sake of being fast.

The moment you enter the world of any successful organization (team), you feel everyone doing their job the best they can for the good of the team. It is an attitude. It's "one for all and all for one." Each individual doing his job while supporting his colleague (teammate). This is no accident. It starts at the top. The head coach sets the tempo. Coaches set tempo by example. It is not a quality you can easily pinpoint. You can coach with an SOU, a singleness of purpose, at high tempo using your own personality. Coaches are all different in their own way. Great coaches are intense and uptempo, using their own style. Some are emotional; some are not. Some are loud; some are quiet. They have one commonality. When they talk, people listen. Great coaches are not good gossipers. They have too much work to do.

Lou Holtz: The Picture of Intense

The quote by Lou Holtz at the beginning of this chapter is telling. Do you recall how he used to complete 14 miles of walking during the course of a game. Posture upright, serious face, constantly stopping and reversing his direction. Not just walking, he was going 96 mph. He had SOU written all over him. That was him. That was his style and he was very successful using it.

Supercharge Your Attitude and Watch Others Follow

You can find plenty of ways to supercharge your team/organization. Adding/increasing your own enthusiasm will cause others to do the same. Increase your SOU and singleness of purpose while using your own personality. Players and coaches will feed off your sense of purpose and enthusiasm. SOU and tempo is the manner in which the entire organization approaches every task necessary for collective success. Take a business approach; sprinkle it with levity. Ask the same from your support staff. Your staff will get things done and have a good laugh once in a while.

Be the Leader

Be a head coach. Rise above petty circumstances. Don't let your staff get bogged down in gossip. Control what you can, and don't look back. Don't allow staff to waste precious preparation time discussing topics that do not prepare you for victory. Assistant coaches sometimes like to "stop at every dog that barks" when they need to be "delivering the mail." Demand that conversations around the office be positive and constructive. You are there to solve problems and help your players. Public issues should not mingle with team issues. You are not at the office to respond to public issues. You are there to discuss football team matters. Discussions about what is in the newspaper, what a parent said, or the like should not be the topic of conversation. These types of conversations serve absolutely no useful purpose.

Coaches should be brutally honest with each other, and then leave it in the office. What happens in the office stays in the office. There is team info and public info. Team info stays in the office. Public info stays in the public.

Increase Your Rate

When coaching the SNH, you have times when players are standing (walk-throughs) or even sitting (meetings, film review). Not much physical is going on. You will have times when you want your team at full speed, both mentally and physically, but you will also have times when you may want just their minds fast (film study and position meetings) with their bodies at rest. This doesn't mean their activities are not high-tempo or are performed without an SOU. Rate is the speed and intensity with which you impart useful information. How you communicate is more important than what you communicate. *How* you say something is perceived more than *what* you say. SOU may simply come in the form of requiring your players to be dressed appropriately and being on time: hustle between drills, getting lined up correctly in a good stance, communication with teammates, and so forth. Your players and coaches will play/coach at the tempo you set.

USC Practice Revelation

I observed Pete Carroll and his coaching staff at a USC practice. I was blown away. *Every* administrator, coach, trainer, manager, filmer, ball placer, field maintenance staff, and so on was high-tempo. Literally every coach at every drill was prodding his players to go faster, try harder, or use better technique. Every drill was a competition, pitting coach versus player, player versus player, coach versus coach, position group versus position group, position group versus coach. Turn your head at any time, and you observed a player either competing with another player in a drill or competing with the guy across from him in team and/or scrimmage situation. Coach Carroll bounced around practice like he was the happiest, luckiest, guy in the world—shouting one minute, whispering the next, constantly exhorting and challenging. Coaches and players tried harder when he was in close proximity. His enthusiasm, his tempo, was contagious.

The Man, The Look

The only thing my high school coach Marijon Ancich had to do was give us a look. He was called "the man," and his look spoke volumes. When you received the look, you knew you had done something very wrong, and it better change immediately. He is one of the most intense, competitive, loyal, high-tempo persons I have ever met. He did it without screaming and yelling. He did raise his voice occasionally, but that was few and far between. He didn't knock over desks or throw clipboards. He didn't do it by demeaning players. He created a sense of purpose and sense of urgency by the way he approached every facet of his job. His SOU and tempo was unmatched when it came to organizing his coaches, practices, workouts, scouting reports, rehab schedules, everything. Coach Ancich is the second-winningest coach in the history of the state of California, with 360 wins. You don't win that many games competing in the competitive Southern Section of California without a sense of urgency.

I heard Coach Jeff Tedford speak when he first took over the program at Cal. It was a small Cal alumni group gathered in Carmel, California. I learned a great deal from listening to him speak that night, but one thing he mentioned stuck with me. One of his first priorities as the new coach at Cal was to make his players aware of their voice, posture, and stride. He said, "Winners walk and talk differently than non-winners." He demonstrated how winners walk a little taller with their chin up and spoke more energetically and positively than non-winners. He talked about the importance of body language and positive voice inflection. He wanted every person in the program to examine the way they walk, talk, and communicate with each other. This is SOU in another form.

"Do not confuse activity with achievement"

John Wooden's quote is remarkably true. More is not necessarily better. It simply means that if you approach your daily activities in a lackadaisical, nonchalant manner, then you shouldn't be surprised if your players play that way. Players feed off your energy. They feed off the tone of your voice and inflexions, the way you walk, the language you use, the goals you set, and various other conscious and unconscious stimuli you present to them. Tempo, as defined by the first sentence of this chapter, is not only the rate of your activities, but also the rhythm and pattern of your work. If you instruct with intensity, then your players will generally react to your instructions intensely. The pattern in which you coach is vitally important. Every activity must be interpreted as a task necessary to get better.

Shalom Ormsby/Blend Images/Thinkstock

*"Spectacular achievements
are always preceded by
unspectacular preparation."*

—Roger Staubach

Build Conditioning Into Practice

Why do coaches feel the need to run gassers and/or wind sprints at the end of practice? If your players give every bit of effort they can during practice, why do more? Is some decree sent from the coaching gods that says players must do sprints and various other activities after practice to be in game shape? For many years, the routine of lining up on the goal line at the end of practice and doing conditioning was the norm. Few ever considered doing it at the beginning or middle of practice, and even fewer considered not doing it at all. It is a routine that has been ingrained into the psyche of coaches everywhere. Most coaches played football. Older generation coaches will tell you how they were asked to get on the goal line by their coaches at the end of practice.

If your players don't give a great effort at practice, then, by all means, get 'em on the line. When players know that they will not have a structured type of run at the end of practice if they hustle and do everything at full speed during practice, they will practice harder. Even your players who don't mind running will appreciate breaking the monotony of lining up on the same line, running the same gassers every day. Formal conditioning drills have their time and place. That is a given. This chapter is talking about in-season conditioning, where your players change daily due to many factors, or you have crucial players who need rest during a long season. Coaches don't intentionally want to make their players feel like they are not in shape by running sprints at the end or middle of practice, but they still do it.

Tempo Is a Natural Conditioner

The great thing about the no-huddle offense is that the tempo of your practice will be so much faster that you will not need to run sprints at the end of practice for your players to be in game shape. Many of you reading this right now may disagree. To coaches who don't run the no-huddle: how would you know if you've never run a practice at no-huddle pace? To those who run a no-huddle offense: are you taking full advantage of the pace and tempo that the no-huddle can give you? Along with running the no-huddle attack comes a more intense and/or aggressive mindset about how you approach your practice. If you approach every drill, group period, and team period with a fast-paced teaching, demanding style, then your players don't need to run sprints at the end of practice. The no-huddle offense is great in this respect. You can practice at game tempo. Imagine how your players feel. They will love you for *not* saying "Okay, everybody on the goal line" at the end of a tough, high-paced practice. Being in shape means not only in great physical condition, but mental condition as well.

A Time for Talking and a Time for Tempo

There is a time during practice to slow down and "talk and walk" through formations and assignments. This valuable time should definitely take place before fast-tempo group or team drills. Try to get these slow-paced periods in at the beginning or before practice so that when you do get into group or team periods, you don't have a lot of explaining and conversation going on. You must create a distinct difference between a walk-through period and a fast-paced drill session.

You will get a much better effort out of your players if they know that they will not be asked to run just for the sake of running after they have busted their butt during practice. This concept of not running conditioning sprints at the end of practice may be new to some of you. The following ideas might help you incorporate conditioning into your practice. The beauty of this is your players will feel like all they are doing is participating in a fast paced practice when they are actually being conditioned mentally and physically.

Two-Minute Drill

Executing the two-minute drill is the most game-like conditioning drill you can run. Think about all the phases of the game you are incorporating, not to mention the fact that you are doing it at the end of practice when your players should be fatigued mentally and physically. Execute the two-minute drill as conditioning on air. You are doing this drill at the end of the practice when the players are tired, so you don't want to run the risk of getting someone hurt by banging with the defense. Start the drill in the huddle so the quarterback can give his two-minute instructions, and then break into full-speed two-minute drill tempo. The players get to their positions quickly after each play and receive the signals from the coach. Tell the wide receivers that you will be in a trips to the field alignment so they know exactly what direction to start heading after the previous play. Call plays that the team will successfully execute.

Don't stop to take a breather when a player goes out-of-bounds. This is a conditioning drill, so act as though there is no out-of-bounds to speed up the drill. If they practice as though they will never get a chance to catch their breath then when they are executing the two-minute drill in the game and go out-of-bounds, they will feel as though they have a ton of time to catch their breath. There is absolutely no stopping the drill to coach. Any mistakes that need to be corrected are done after the drill. Call runs that the team is comfortable with and pass plays that are likely to be completed. This drill is great to condition the team physically for a game-like two-minute drill as well as build their confidence in executing the plays when they are tired. Insist that your players execute their assignments perfectly. They must learn to be perfect when their bodies and minds want to quit.

Make sure you have a coach assigned to mark the ball after every snap. Tell this coach to give you, the play caller, all different sorts of down-and-distance situations. Don't script this drill. By not scripting this drill, you also condition your play caller to think fast and come up with a good play under time and game pressure. This is a form of mental conditioning for the play caller to coach on the run in the two-minute drill.

Screen Drill

The screen is another game-like drill that allows you to determine precisely how much running your team will actually do for conditioning. It doesn't matter whether it is a running back screen or wide receiver screen; the entire team runs 40 yards downfield after the catch is made. This forces the quarterback to make the touch throws while he is tired, the receiver to catch the ball, as well as force your linemen to execute their assignment and run a full 40 yards in leading your receiver downfield. This is practicing a real back-breaker for the defense. Nothing is more demoralizing to a defense in the two-minute drill than to rush the passer when they are tired only to have the offense run a screen. The defensive linemen must stop, retrace their path, and chase down a receiver 40 yards downfield. This not only tires the defense physically, it frustrates them mentally. It is a statistical fact that screens can be your highest percentage passes in the passing game. Using them in a conditioning drill gives everybody involved a sense of how far they may have to run when executing a back-breaking screen play. Having a lineman turn around to watch a ballcarrier or assuming the play is over rather than running downfield to block someone are the two biggest mistakes that occur on screen plays. This drill forces everyone involved to turn screen plays into long gainers. You can have your first, second, and third teams going rapid fire, one after the other. It allows you to closely monitor how far your offensive team runs because you start from one spot and require them to run specifically 40 yards. This is one drill where you can involve the defense if you want. Tell your defensive linemen to rush the quarterback even if they know it is a screen. Require that they rush the quarterback, get fooled, and sprint 40 yards to catch the ballcarrier.

"So in war, the way is to avoid what is strong and to strike at what is weak."

—Sun Tzu

Identifying the Fish Out of Water

Finding the fish out of water (FOW) is not the same as finding their weakest player. The FOW is the player that, because of his alignment and/or assignment, is being asked to perform tasks of which he is not capable. He is the player that as a result of your offensive formation is put in a position of weakness by the mere fact that he doesn't know what to do or he doesn't have the physical ability to do it. Either way, you want to find him and attack him. It's a bonus when the opponent's fish out of water is also their weakest player, but that's not always the case. Only by rigorous film work can you find the kinks in the defensive armor, but it is time well spent when you can help your players be the best they can be by putting them in game situations that match their strengths to the defense's weaknesses. The optimum situation is for you to not only find the fish out of water (FOW), but to match your team's particular strengths to that individual.

"Be what he isn't."

—Hans Schmidt

This quote by the great basketball coach Hans Schmidt says it most succinctly. Find the FOW, match him with your strength, and then "Be what he isn't."

Same Stuff, Different Look

Defenses are very assignment-oriented. Players are coached to line up in a specific way against specific formations, which means the offense can at times, by formation, dictate where the defense will line up. The offensive coach must use this to his advantage. You don't have to change your offense to attack an FOW. Simply lining up in a vanilla formation at first to see where the defense lines up is a great starting point. See where your FOW lines up, and have ways prepared to put your best offensive weapon on him or run your best plays at him. By no means should you feel the need to develop new plays to attack the FOW. Good teams do all the little things consistently well. Running the same basic plays out of different looks should not detract from the vitally important assignments inherent to the success of the play. You are not changing the purpose, scope, or design of the play. You are running the same plays, but with small but very important variances that cause confusion, force a mismatch, or gain a man advantage at the point of attack.

The Good Old Days

Historically, defenses were originally designed to stop a conventional 21 personnel offense with at least two backs and one tight end. The FOW was easy to locate. He was the player who, by the nature of his position, (a position designed to stop 21 personnel), was put at a disadvantage when the tight end was displaced to become a wide receiver or the running back left the backfield to align as a wide receiver. When you present them with no tight end and only one back, you force them to adjust into an alignment to which they may not be accustomed or for which they lack the personnel. In the past, high school base defenses were not set up to handle more than two wide receivers.

If you examine the traditional 5-2 cover 2, you will see that when you spread this defense out at least one of their defenders must play an assignment that they don't normally play or takes on an assignment at which he is physically deficient. This defender is either strong at stopping the run and is a weak pass defender, or vice versa. Maybe he is a defender whose position is normally on the line of scrimmage, but because of your spread formation he is displaced into the secondary. In Figures 12-1 through 12-3, the FOW will be the player in a square.

5-2 vs. 21 Personnel (Figure 12-1)

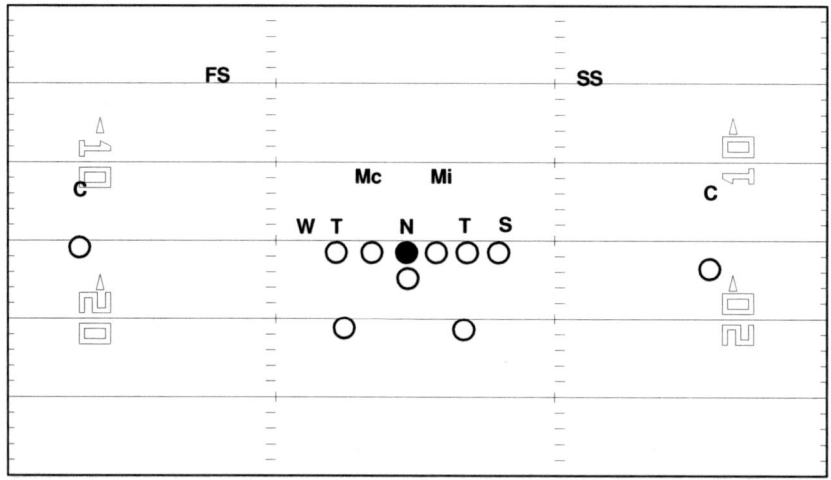

Figure 12-1. 5-2 vs. 21 personnel

This play is the typical 5-2 50 defense matched against 21 personnel (two running backs, one tight end).

5-2 Cover 2 vs. Double Slot (Figure 12-2)

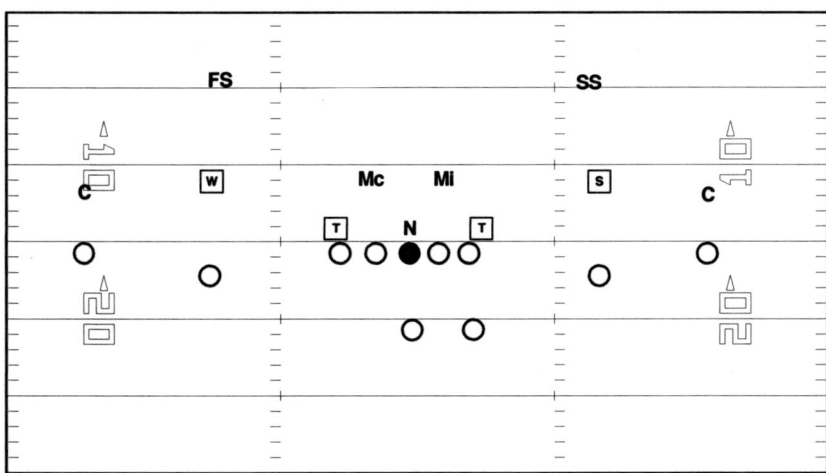

Figure 12-2. 5-2 cover 2 vs. double slot

This play is that same 50 defense versus a double slot formation.

- S is now out in space aligned against a wide receiver rather than playing off a tight end as a run stopper.
- W is also displaced covering a wide receiver. He likes being at the end of the line of scrimmage, closer to the action.
- The Ts may potentially be outside rushers. They are used to having a defensive end right there on their hip.

5-2 Cover 3 vs. Trips (Figure 12-3)

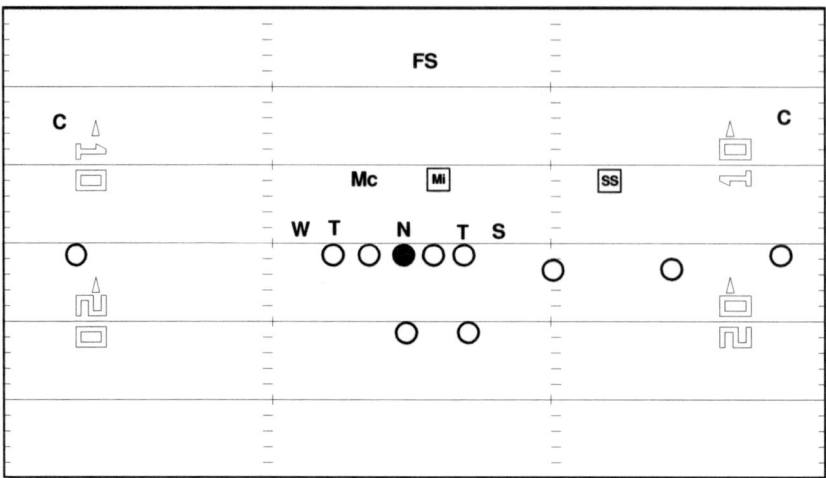

Figure 12-3. 5-2 cover 3 vs. trips

- The Mike linebacker is put in a very precarious situation. He has gap run responsibilities as well as hook-to-curl to the strongside. They are playing with seven players in the box. The scheme is an FOW. Sprint and/or max protect, and throw the ball.

Figures 12-4 through 12-9 identify the potential FOW when lining up in trips and double slot formations versus cover 2, cover 3, and quarters coverage.

Trips vs. Cover 3 (Figure 12-4)

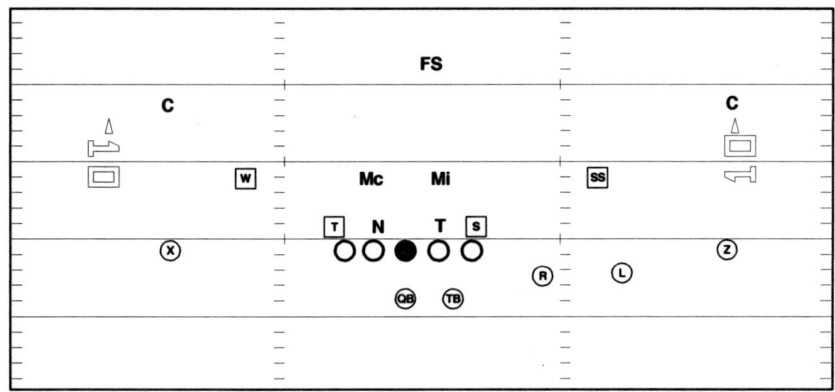

Figure 12-4. Trips vs. cover 3

- SS is playing in space with two wide receivers to threaten him, not just one.
- Mike (Mi) has that same problem of being responsible for inside run and hook-to-curl to the strongside. With a big split by #3 wide receiver, he is in deep trouble.
- S is now playing on a man rather than air. He now has pass rush responsibilities rather than curl-flat pass duties.
- T is all alone at the end of the line due to W linebacker being displaced. He now has outside pass rush responsibilities as well as edge run support.
- W is now in space rather than a stand-up defensive end.

Trips vs. Cover 2 (Figure 12-5)

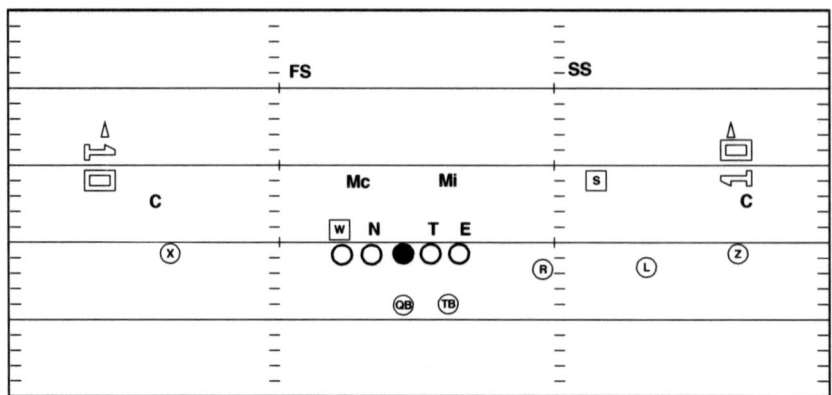

Figure 12-5. Trips vs. cover 2

- S is in unfamiliar territory. He didn't sign up to be a defensive back. He is a run stopper who is being asked to do something with which he is uncomfortable. He is wondering, "What are all these receivers doing out here?"
- W is playing on a man rather than air. He has pass rush responsibilities rather than curl-flat pass duties.

Trips vs. Quarters Coverage (Figure 12-6)

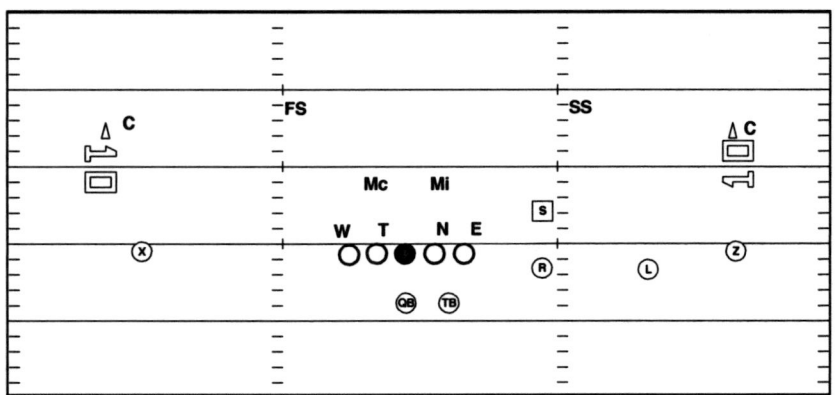

Figure 12-6. Trips vs. quarters coverage

- S may not be the best man-to-man cover player. He must stay with a tight end to the flat or reroute if the tight end crosses his face.

Double Slot vs. Cover 3 (Figure 12-7)

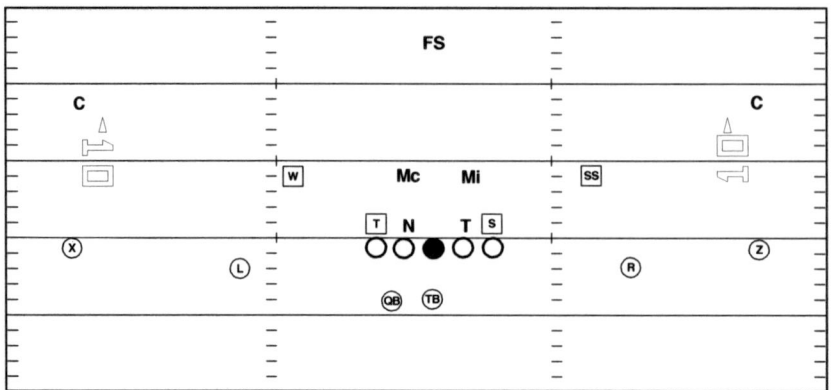

Figure 12-7. Double slot vs. cover 3

- SS is playing in space with two wide receivers to threaten him, not just one.
- S is playing on a man rather than air. He is possibly being asked to get in a three-point stance, which puts him in another world. Some very athletic players become average when you change their stance from a two-point to a three-point and vice versa. Evolution has made humans more comfortable standing up. S now has pass rush *and* run responsibilities rather than curl-flat pass duties.
- T is all alone at the end of the line due to W linebacker being displaced. He now has outside pass rush responsibilities as well as edge run support.
- W is playing in space rather than a stand-up defensive end.

Double Slot vs. Cover 2 (Figure 12-8)

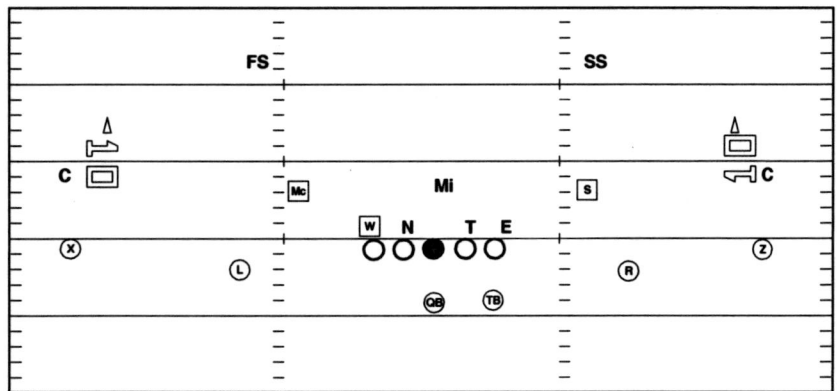

Figure 12-8. Double slot vs. cover 2

- S is in unfamiliar territory. He didn't sign up to be a defensive back. He is a run stopper who is being asked to do something with which he is not comfortable. He is saying, "What are all these receivers doing out here?"
- W is now playing on a man rather than air. He now has pass rush responsibilities rather than curl-flat pass duties.
- Mc is very displaced. He is not an out on air kind of guy. He likes it better between the tackles.

Double Slot vs. Quarters Coverage (Figure 12-9)

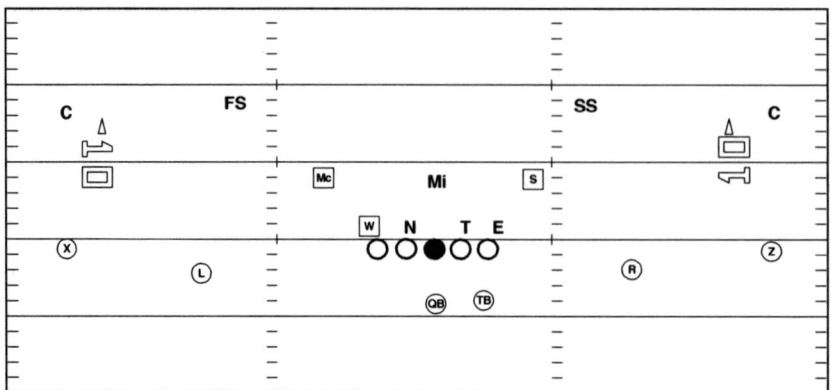

Figure 12-9. Double slot vs. quarters coverage

- S may not be the best man-to-man cover player. He must stay with a tight end to the flat or reroute if the tight end crosses his face.
- W is playing on a man rather than air. He has pass rush responsibilities rather than curl-flat pass duties.
- Mc is very displaced. He is not an out on air kind of guy. He likes it better between the tackles.

The New Question With 3-4 and 3-5 Defenses: Can He Stop Run *and* Pass?

Finding weak personnel becomes critical when facing 3-4 and 3-5 defenses. The weakness in the defense may not be as obvious vs. the 3-5 and 3-4 defense as it is with the 5-2, 4-4, and 4-3. Some hybrid linebackers are not equipped to be the run stopper or pass defender they are asked to be. Some hybrid players lack the physicality to stop inside run plays but can pass cover and vice versa. He is not as conspicuous as in the past. Three down linemen versus the spread formation means teams are playing with more non-linemen than ever before. These are not nickel or dime substitutes. They are who they are. The defensive coach may have them out there because that's the best he has. The ideal situation is to find the hybrid strong safety or linebacker that is too small to be a defensive lineman and too slow to be a defensive back or his body type is more suited to a two-point stance but he can't tackle. Those three linemen better be pretty good because a good SNH team will slam it down your throat with a power running game. Figures 12-10 through 12-13 illustrate the potential FOW when trips and double slot are matched against 3-4 and 3-5 defenses.

3-4 vs. Trips (Figure 12-10)

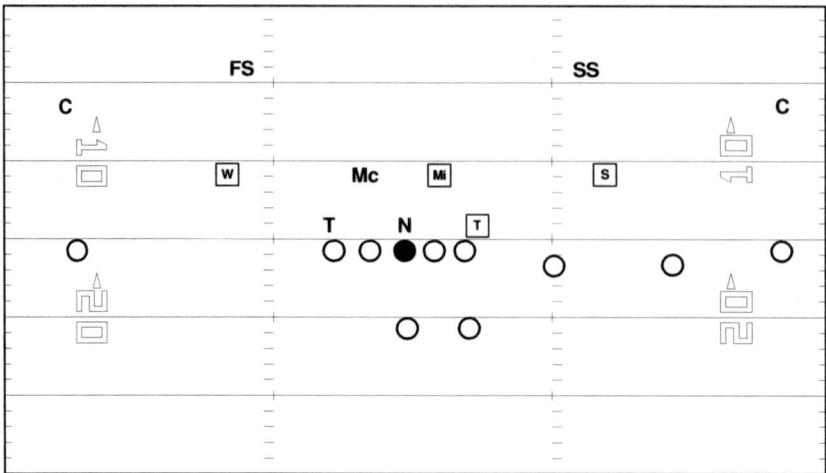

Figure 12-10. 3-4 vs. trips

- T is now all alone at the end of the line due to W linebacker being displaced. He now has outside pass rush responsibilities as well as edge run support.
- S and W are hybrid players that may lack the physical tools to be effective run stoppers as well as pass defenders. These players are sometimes used as rushers, but lack the size or speed to do much damage.
- Mi is in a very tough position to defend hook-to-curl to the strongside.
- W is a hybrid player who may be deficient at run or pass assignments.

If you are going to play with only three down linemen, they better be pretty good unless your scheme inserts a fourth or fifth man into the line of scrimmage or your linebacking corps is exceptional.

3-4 vs. Double Slot (Figure 12-11)

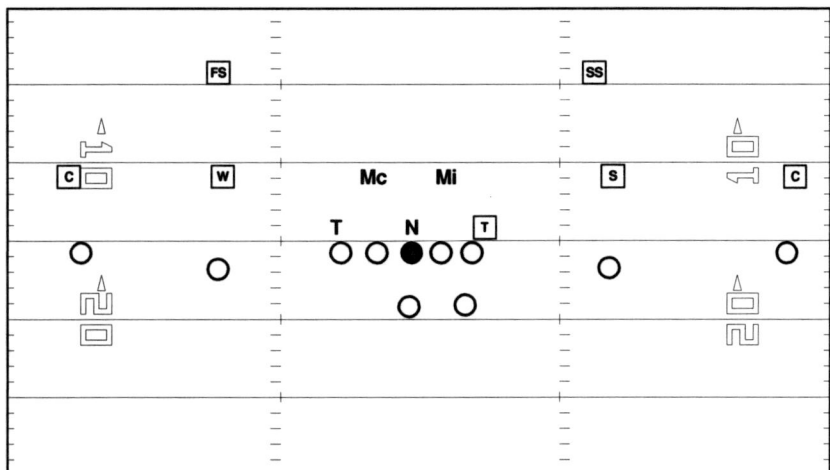

Figure 12-11. 3-4 vs. double slot

- S and W are hybrid players that may lack the physical tools to be effective run stoppers as well as pass defenders. These players are sometimes used as rushers but lack the size or speed to do much damage. It is rare to find an S or W that is good at both tackling and pass cover.
- T is all alone at the end of the line due to W linebacker being displaced. He now has outside pass rush responsibilities as well as edge run support.

3-5 vs. Trips (Figure 12-12)

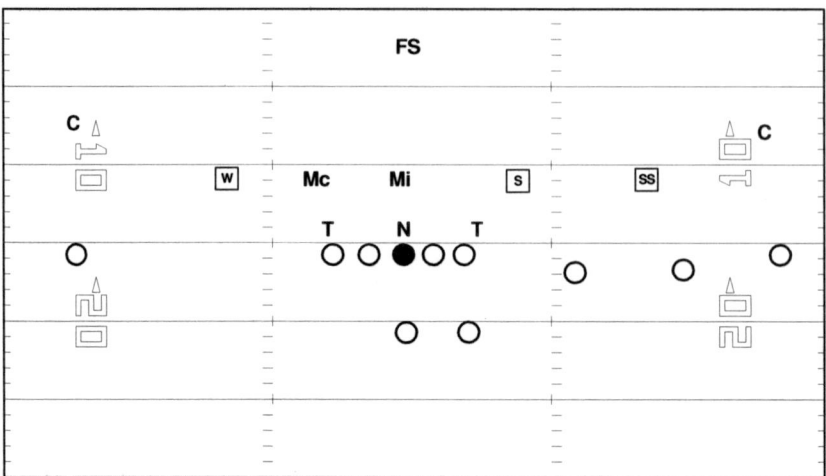

Figure 12-12. 3-5 vs. trips

- S and W are hybrid players that may lack the physical tools to be effective run stoppers as well as pass defenders. These players are sometimes used as rushers, but lack the size or speed to do much damage.
- SS is playing in space with two wide receivers to threaten him, not just one.

3-5 vs. Double Slot (Figure 12-13)

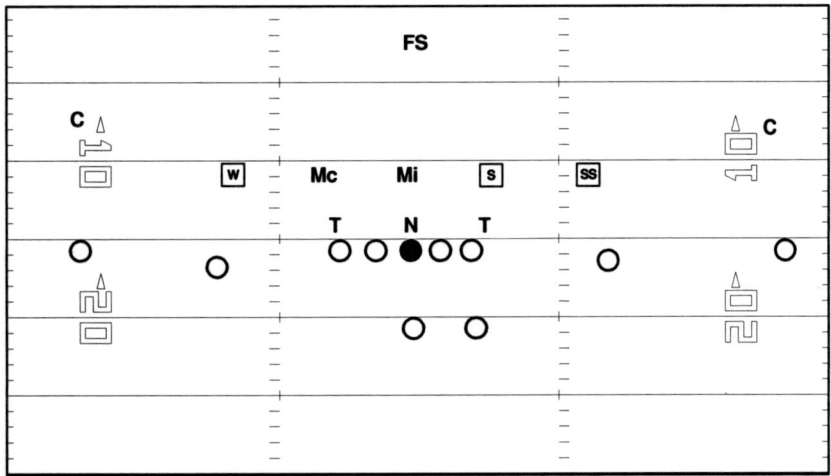

Figure 12-13. 3-5 vs. double slot

- Mc and S are forced to be run stoppers if W and SS are displaced.
- W may be a weak pass or perimeter run defender.
- SS may lack the ability to cover the flat for an entire two-thirds of the field.

*"Practice without improvement
is meaningless."*

—Chuck Knox

Maximize Practice Time

How many of you conduct the same practice whether it is the third day of spring or the 10th week of the season? Do you run the same drills at the same time every day? Have you ever imagined what it's like for your players who must anticipate the same practice routine day in and day out? Much is to be said for repeating the same techniques and terms daily, but when does the repetition become inflexible and/or monotonous?

Winners Prioritize Time

In order to supercharge your existing practice techniques, you must think of ways out of the box to make practice more purposeful and relevant. What, when, and how you practice should be determined based on what you think necessary to beat your next opponent. That's it. Practicing with a purpose means that every activity during practice contributes to better game-time performance. What good is it to spend practice time performing drills or executing plays that you are not going to run in the game? Take a serious look at how your practice time is allocated. You may find that you practice stuff you don't run at all. Practicing with purpose forces you to reflect on what you do at practice and ask yourself if what you're practicing is going to be called in the game and how much. Then ask yourself if you are really allocating enough practice time so that when you call it in the game, it is executed successfully. The game of football and how it is practiced is constantly evolving and improving. Purposeful practice is what is appropriate for your team at that moment in time. Weird stuff can happen over the course of a season that can affect what and how you practice. Your opponent, injuries, game plans, ineligible players, weather, daylight, and such are common variables that occur during a football season. Maybe it is not appropriate to practice in full gear three times a week for a week 10 game. Coaching 110 players on a college team is much different than coaching an enthusiastic group of 35 high schoolers.

Practice With Purpose

"You can't make a great play unless you do it first in practice."

—Chuck Noll

In the dictionary, the opposite of purposeful is *aimless*. You don't want to aimlessly go through practice every day. Practicing plays and/or techniques that won't be utilized in the upcoming game is wasted time. You don't have to put all your eggs in one basket and throw out 95 percent of your offense. It simply means that you get good at what you think will work *that week*. Decide what it's going to take to come up at least one point ahead of the other guy, and practice that. This is *game* week practice. You have run many different plays from the beginning of spring practice to now. It is time to eliminate plays and fine tune or tweak what matches your opponent. If, by film study, you see that the defense will give you an opportunity to throw a post pattern for a touchdown on Friday night, then practice the heck out of the post pattern that week. If you will face a corner who is susceptible to the out route, then practice that more than the routes that won't be called. Don't throw out everything. Allocate more practice time to what you are going to attempt and less time on things you won't.

Specific players run specific routes in your offense. Get your players good at what they will be asked to do. If the quarterback is going to throw that post pattern discussed earlier, then have him practice it with the players he will be throwing to. It is with those guys that the timing and execution need to be ironed out. Having everyone in the offense practice the post route is useless. Players should be given time to perfect those skills inherent to the specific position they play and the plays they will run in the game.

Adjust Existing Attack

Adjust blocking schemes and assignments to a few basic plays instead of trying to block every play in the playbook. Make an educated assumption of what the defense has in store for you, and choose the best way to attack it. Fine-tune your scheme so you get good at the specific things that work best against that opponent. For example, practice blocking 26 power with three different blocking calls specific to that opponent rather than throwing it out in the first place because it wasn't perfect against that defense. Make small variations to what your bread-and-butter plays are, and eliminate those you have no intention of calling.

Make up calls specific to that week. The players enjoy learning new stuff that will help them win. They will memorize these calls easily because of their sense of novelty and the fact that you are going to hammer them into their head all week during every film session, meeting, walk-through, and practice. These special calls could give you some great blocking angles with your offensive line and/or sight adjust routes with your wide receivers on Friday night.

Improved Game and Practice Tempo

Huddling up after every play is the biggest waste of time and energy in the game of football. The notion that a huddle facilitates better cohesion and communication within an offensive team is nonsense. Think about how much unnecessary practice time and energy it takes for players to run back to the huddle after a play, receive the new play from the quarterback, and then run back out to their position to execute the next play. Notice the time it gives the defense to regroup, recover, and prepare for the next play. Cohesion and communication within an offensive football team is something that is developed from hours and hours of organized, high-tempo, meaningful practice. Huddling is not necessary.

The beautiful thing about the no-huddle scheme is not only the advantages it gives you in actual games, but also in practice. Do you break your practices up into neatly timed periods and assume that you are getting an adequate amount of repetitions? If you were to take a stopwatch and calculate the time you presently spend getting in and out of a huddle during practice and compare that with a high-tempo no-huddle practice, the hard facts will tell you that you can run more plays in less time. Solid data will tell you how much time you may be wasting getting in and out of the huddle during team and group drills. You can get twice as much done in practice in about half the time. When you couple a slow-tempo practice with the need to huddle after every play, then you will either have to stay at practice longer or leave on time and not accomplish what needs to get done. If you don't run the SNH offense presently, you will be amazed at how many more plays and how much more coaching you can get done when you incorporate it into your practice.

The following are tried and proven ways to improve your quality of practice and shorten the time you need to spend on the practice field:

- *Eliminate down time.* No one gets better standing for long periods. Rest periods are necessary, but movement and action foster improvement.
- *Keep players getting better while they watch.* Wide receivers with a ball in their hands at all times. Running backs alternating tucking the ball under each armpit with the five points of pressure. Centers taking shotgun snaps with quarterbacks, and so on.
- *Repeat key words rather than long explanations.* Key words can be repeated easily and forcefully. Key words facilitate quick, clear communication that aids practice instruction and the crucial transmission of information during a game.
- *Talk fast and confidently.* Show energy, enthusiasm, and confidence in your voice, and your players will respond accordingly. Practice is not the time for long, slow, unenergetic explanations. Don't break the rhythm of a practice or drill by talking. Players get better when they are doing. Talk less; do more.
- *Organize a smooth flowing practice.* No matter your method of implementation, try to help the player transition from one drill to another with learning and improvement in mind. Make your practice flow in such a way that there is a progression of learning and executing taking place. Part-part-whole, whole-part-whole, you choose. Make it logical, and make it flow.

- *Insist on quick transition between periods.* Require that your coaches and players get to the next drill quickly. Assistant coaches should have bags or other drill accessories set up prior to the drill. Quick transition from drill to drill not only saves valuable practice time, it creates a sense of urgency.
- *Make checklists.* You want to be able to coach fast and on the run. Checklists help you make sure you're covering the plays you want to see against the defenses you anticipate facing.
- *Practice game tempo.* Your players will play the game at the tempo you make them practice. If you practice slow and lethargic, you will play that way.
- *Signal plays.* Even if your players are two feet from you, use signals. Constant repetition of signals is necessary for good communication during the game. Make your players vocalize what you are signaling. Every player either in the drill or watching must say the play as the coach signals it.
- *Don't interrupt fast-paced drills with explanations.* Substitute fast and avoid stopping the drill to explain anything. Explain after practice or your next film session.

You, as a coach, will surely organize your practices as you see fit. The goal is to give you general ideas of some concepts that have been very successful and leave it up to you to find the time to insert them into your practice planning. The most important thing you can do, whether you are just beginning to implement an SNH attack or are currently using it, is to see where you can avoid the standing around that takes place between plays at practice. You must be a fanatic about tempo in practice! A team that practices intensely and with high tempo during practice plays the game the same way.

Dedicate Time to Talk-and-Walk Game Plan

Too many coaches waste high-tempo team periods by stopping the action to instruct players. It may seem contradictory to discuss a talk-and-walk period when the goal is to have a fast-paced, high-tempo practice, but it is necessary. The goal of the talk-and-walk period is to get all or most of the mental work involved in your offense done before you go to a team period. When you are in a team period, you shouldn't give an inordinate amount of instruction that will slow the pace of a polish-type drill. This is facilitated by allocating a period of your practice time to talk and walk through assignments that your players will be performing. This period should take place before or early in the practice. This talk-and-walk period should not be done after you have stretched and warmed up. You don't want to waste a good warm-up when the players' blood is flowing to stop and talk through assignments.

Your talk should be concise, and your walk should be brisk. You must devote time to teach your players what they could potentially see in the game and answer any questions they might have before asking them to execute in a full-speed team drill. If your players are given certain rules that dictate what specific assignments they have on any given play, then it needs explaining. Your talk-and-walk period is devoted to showing your players what defense they can expect to see that week and how their rules will apply. Any questions regarding their assignment are answered during this period. The players will appreciate the fact that you are spending valuable practice time to clearly show them what to expect and explaining to them what your expectations are regarding their assignments. The goal of these talk-and-walk periods is to avoid the talking and walking later in practice when you are in a high-tempo team period.

Coach Groups Before Team Periods

Break up your offensive team into two groups when conducting a talk-and-walk period: one group would include offensive linemen, running backs, and quarterbacks, and the second group would be wide receivers versus a scout secondary. The first group (offensive linemen, running backs, quarterbacks) would be talking and walking versus the defensive front seven, solving blocking and possible audible assignments, while the second group (wide receivers) will be introduced to coverages and blitz sight adjustments they can anticipate that week. The goal is to solve all the mental situations before you jump into a team period. You can even break up your group period to focus on just one phase or another (e.g., the run game or just blitz pick-up). You want to be specific in these periods. Don't bother the players with plays that you will not be running that Friday night. This is your time to make sure that your offense will be prepared for the specific fronts, blitzes, and coverages that you expect to see. The goal is to have your players confident at game time, so you must do your homework before you get in your group and instruct your players. You should present your plan with confidence and enthusiasm so the players will feel like the plan has been thought through, and if they execute, the team will be successful. The players will feed off your positive demeanor. Players are smart. They will sense any uncertainty on your part. Make the players believe in the plan. Make them feel as though you have developed a great game plan. They will appreciate this. You are telling your players that you have done your part to analyze the opponent, and now it is up to them to execute the plan.

Individual 1-on-1 Drills

Individual 1-on-1 drills are good because they allow the player, regardless of his position, to execute his skills against an opponent without a bunch of bodies flying around him. You get good, physical technique work in without the risk of another player rolling into an ankle or knee. Examples of types of 1-on-1 drills can include:
- Offensive linemen vs. defensive linemen pass and run blocking
- Tight end vs. outside linebacker pass and run blocking and pass routes
- Guards vs. linebackers pass and run blocking
- Running backs vs. defensive end or inside linebacker sprint protection
- Running backs vs. inside linebacker blitz blocking
- Running backs vs. inside linebacker or outside linebacker pass routes
- Wide receivers vs. defensive backs pass routes

The 1-on-1 drills should be done prior to any team drills. Make sure to mix up the snap count when performing any blocking drills. As discussed in Chapter 7, it is imperative to practice changing the snap count. It must become ingrained in your players through repetition that the snap count will be different nearly every play. You want to make the drills as game-like as possible. The biggest advantage 1-on-1 drills give you is having the offensive player isolated with a defensive player without the chance of an injury occurring from another player adjacent to him. It also gives the coach an opportunity to work on specific weaknesses the player may have. Be sure to film the 1-on-1 drill so you can let the player see exactly where he is making mistakes with technique and the like.

7-on-7 Drills

This is a great period to sharpen up the passing game. Make sure to include a real center in the drill to ensure that your quarterback is required to catch the snap, get his hands on the threads, place the ball in a throwing position, make his reads, and deliver the ball with proper footwork and balance. The offensive team should consist of everybody but the offensive linemen. The defensive team should consist of all defensive players except defensive linemen. Assign a scout team coach to make sure the defense is set up in the alignments that you anticipate your opponent will run. You are not huddling, so you must have a coach that signals in the plays. Tempo is essential. You cannot expect your players to play at a high tempo in the game unless you conduct your drills as such. Script your plays so that the ball is moved from hash to hash. After the signal is given from coach to players, you must make sure that everyone involved gets to their proper landmarks quickly. It is imperative that your wide receivers get the signal and space themselves out appropriately for the specific play that was called (see Chapter 16). Make sure that your players are in the proper alignment to ensure proper execution of the play. Too many coaches put the ball in the middle of the field every play during practice. This is not realistic at all. In the game, the ball is rarely right in the middle of the field. At least 70 to 80 percent of the time the ball is on a hash. This is the time in practice that spacing and execution of the passing game and tempo are defined.

This skelly drill is one of the most important drills that you will conduct during your practice. You must coach on the run and insist that your players execute the play properly. Players must get the next signal from the coach early, and use their landmarks to get ready to execute the next play. This drill incorporates many of the important factors inherent to a successful spread no-huddle attack: communication from coach to players, players knowledge of what their assignment is, using landmarks appropriate to the play, and tempo are all practiced in this drill.

Full-Team Game Tempo

This part of practice is when you put it all together. Every coach has had an opportunity to talk and walk their assignments, work as a group, and conduct 1-on-1 drills with their respective position groups. This is as close to game conditions as practice can get. This is the *whole* portion of the part, part, whole philosophy of practice implementation. You have covered all the parts, so now it is time to execute as a whole football team. It is vitally important that you not disrupt the tempo or flow of this part of practice by stopping to coach your players. If you need to correct or coach a player, you should pull him out of the drill and replace him. *Do not slow this drill down with an inordinate amount of teaching!* You had plenty of opportunity to teach and instruct your players during the drills prior to this team period. If and when you do any coaching during this period, it should be fast and concise. This is not the period to introduce new concepts or techniques. It should be a polish period with an emphasis on tempo and execution.

In order for this period to accomplish what it is intended for, you must make sure that your scout team coach is getting the defense ready to handle the no-huddle speed. This is the period that the no-huddle will save you a bunch of time. By not huddling, you should be able to run twice as many plays as you could if you were to huddle between each play. Subs should be near the coach calling the plays, so there is no slow-down when substitutions are made. Coaches can choose a script or call on the run format.

Two-Minute Drill Is "No Big Deal"

Can you imagine how confident your team will be if and when you are called upon to execute the two-minute drill in a game? If you are practicing the no-huddle attack as you should, your players will have run the two-minute drill hundreds of times. It has been their tempo since the first day of spring practice. In fact, they may not even feel different than the first series of the game. Your team will start their two-minute drive excited and feeling 100 percent prepared that they are ready for the moment. The only difference might be that you huddle before the first play of the series so your quarterback can give the generic two-minute drill instructions to your running backs and wide receivers to secure the ball, get out-of-bounds if you can, and look to the quarterback for possible time-outs. This is one of the biggest advantages of the no-huddle offense. Some teams might devote 15 to 20 minutes per week executing the two-minute drill, while you have practiced it at least half of your total practices for the week.

Two-Minute Drill as Conditioning

Many times during the course of a season, you should run the two-minute drill as conditioning during practice. As mentioned in Chapter 11, a fast-paced, high-tempo practice is sufficient to have your players in game shape. It is not necessary to run sprints or gassers. Most players disdain running gassers or wind sprints at the end of practice. When a player gives every bit of effort during practice, it is not necessary to do more to get in game shape. Most coaches don't intentionally want to make their players feel like they are not in shape by running sprints at the end or middle of practice, but they still do it.

The great thing about the no-huddle offense is that the tempo of your practice will be so much faster that you will not need to run sprints at the end of practice for your players to be in game shape. Many of you may be reading this right now that disagree. To those coaches who don't run the no-huddle, how would you know if you've never run a practice at no-huddle pace? To those who run a no-huddle offense, are you taking full advantage of the pace and tempo that the no-huddle can give you?

Running the SNH attack comes with a more intense and/or aggressive mindset about how you approach your practice. If you approach every drill, group period, and team period with a fast-paced teaching, demanding style, then your players don't need to run sprints at the end of practice. The no-huddle offense is great in this respect. You can practice at game tempo. Your players will love you for not saying, "Okay, everybody on the goal line" at the end of a tough, high-paced practice. Imagine how your players feel.

James Pauls/iStock/Thinkstock

"Enter every activity without recognizing defeat. Concentrate on your strengths instead of your weaknesses, on your powers instead of your problems."

—Paul Meyer

Play to Your Strengths

As a football coach at any level, you must play with the players you have. It is dangerous to assume that you can automatically attack defenses the way you did last year. You may have many of the same players as last year, but surely this year is different in some way(s). It may be subtle, or it may be obvious. Every team has its own personality, chemistry, and skill set.

Hard to Find a Strength?

One of the great things about the spread no-huddle offense is that it gives you chances with big, strong, small, weak, fast, slow, tough, not-so-tough, and a lot of combinations of all these traits. The diversity inherent to the SNH offers the coach a wealth of scheme choices. There certainly are enough different types of plays that can accommodate the different skill sets that will be presented to you on a yearly basis at any level. A wide variety of plays utilize the many potential positions within the spread formation. Maybe the strength of your team is your offensive line and running backs, maybe it's quarterback and wide receivers, or maybe it's a little bit of both. You can choose from running plays that attack inside and outside, while you have pass plays that can attack numerous areas of the field from a variety of launch points.

Will You Have an Offensive Emphasis?

A million written and unwritten factors come into play when choosing your offensive emphasis. It is up to you to determine what your players' physical, mental, and psychological abilities are. Based on these factors, you will decide what it is that you are going to do strategically within the spread no-huddle offense. You have many tools in your belt to attack the defense in some way. Creativity coupled with a little common sense will help you choose what players on your team will run what plays. Take a global perspective of your team's abilities, and then determine your specific strengths before deciding what scheme you will use within the spread no-huddle system.

Spread No-Huddle Gives You Choices

With some schemes that do just one thing (e.g., all run vs. all pass), you are out of luck if you don't have the guys who can do it. You should not have this trouble with the spread no-huddle. The spread no-huddle is built on diversity. What started years ago as a predominantly passing scheme has evolved beautifully into a highly malleable and balanced offensive system. By spreading the defense out, you have choices and advantages in both the run and pass game. This flexibility pays off when one year your offensive personnel may dictate running the ball and the next year it's passing the ball. Ideally, you would like to strive for a balanced attack; an attack that matches the strengths of your offensive personnel to a variety of different play choices. It is beautiful to see how some of today's coaches are tweaking the SNH. It is fun to watch the creativeness in which offensive coordinators are playing smash mouth football disguised as an elaborate pass scheme.

In the run game, you have draw, trap, counter, power, pitch sweep, fly sweep, zone read, option, and so forth. In the pass game, you have the quick game, dropback, sprint, bootleg, waggle, play-action, screens, short-intermediate-deep passes. Running a spread no-huddle offense doesn't mean that you can't slam the ball down their throat. Some of the greatest advantages of the spread no-huddle come in the running game.

Great Quarterback, but Inferior Offensive Line?

What do you do when you have a great quarterback and a very mediocre line? Rather than have your quarterback drop back into a pocket and get massacred every play, try spreading out your receivers, making sure you have solid protection to the edge of the line of scrimmage you are sprinting to, and run one-man routes to the X side and two-man routes to the two-wide receiver side. Use a five-wide receiver set, and displace one more interior defender from the box. The quarterback will see what edge is softest in regards to a rush, and sprint to that side.

This example may be a bit simplified, but it gives you an example of how to play to your strengths. It may appear as though the quarterback is, at times, running for his life, but at least you are giving him a fighting chance to make plays by sprinting to a solid perimeter and making easy throws or utilizing his athleticism by pulling the ball down and running. You may have a quarterback throw for over 2,000 yards and run for nearly 1,000 yards. This sprint mentality with an inferior offensive line can be helpful. The reason sprint blocking is preferred over quick 90 game blocking is because it allows your offensive line to get into run block mode and be more aggressive, rather than be asked to set and maintain a hard-charging defensive line in quick or dropback pass protection mode. It is a common mistake to think that you will run the quick passing game and get rid of the ball before the rush gets to the quarterback. The idea is good, but when executed may resemble a jailbreak. With an inferior offensive line, you give them a chance to hold their man a little longer when they can prioritize their head positioning and fire out in a more aggressive manner. In describing this technique, offensive line coach Monte Clark would say: "Don't show your face, don't show your numbers, head priority, hit, climb, wall, stick."

The use of screens, draws, and misdirection-type runs such as trap and counter may also be effective with a weak offensive line. By allowing your offensive linemen to take advantage of their opponents' overaggressiveness by fooling or enticing them occasionally can be helpful. Trap, counter, and double-team blocks should be utilized to give your offensive line angles when blocking superior defensive linemen.

Great Offensive Line and Mediocre Quarterback?

No need to abandon the spread no-huddle. Adjust your offensive philosophy, and establish a strong inside and outside running game. This approach allows you to get into favorable down-and-distance situations and help your quarterback when he does throw. He will be throwing the ball when the defense is less expectant with play-action passes.

"Worry is a futile thing, it's somewhat like a rocking chair, although it keeps you occupied, it doesn't get you anywhere."

—Anonymous

Throw Deep on First Down

Go Deep!

Don't worry about going deep on first down. Don't forget you still have three downs to pick up a first if things don't go as planned. That is the beauty of the SNH offense. One of the biggest obstacles you must overcome when implementing an SNH system is the fear of being stuck in a second-and-10 situation, or worse yet a sack and face a second-and-16. This situation is death for offensive coaches who are used to running the ball on first and second down, and then throwing the ball on third down if necessary. Throwing the ball when the running game isn't working. Not only that, they are now throwing the ball when the defense expects it. Your first down bomb can originate from a play-action or dropback pass. Any pass you throw on first down will force the defense to have to defend every skill player on your offensive team every down.

On First Down

First down is a great down to throw the ball deep. If you complete the deep pass, you gain a huge advantage in momentum and field position. If you don't complete the pass, you still have two or three more downs to pick up a first. Have your quarterback take a couple of steps and heave it deep. Doing so eliminates the risk of a sack, setting up second down and long. Your first down bomb should be a pass that is either complete or incomplete. No sacks! You are informing the defense that they better be aware of not just a pass, but a deep pass. If teams come to expect that you may throw deep on first down, they will align in a defense that is heavy versus the pass. This alignment will enable you to run the ball more effectively. Throw deep on first down occasionally and calculatingly. You might hit the big one. If you don't, you still have more downs and will get the defense to back off a bit. Figure 15-1 illustrates a good play to use on first down to spread the defense and throw deep.

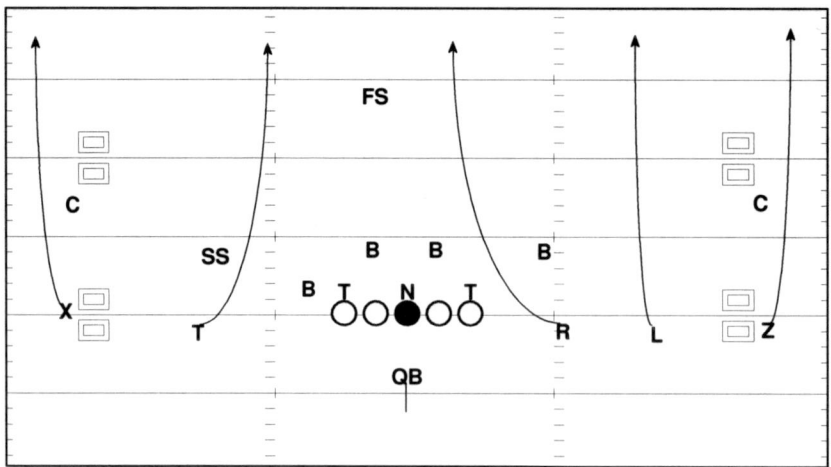

Figure 15-1. Red 79

Assignments:

Q: Increases initial depth by two yards. Three-step drop. Eyes free safety. Throws to open receiver.

T: Splits difference between offensive tackle and X. Gets up the hash, maintaining equal spacing.

X: Gets wide split to stretch free safety. Runs a 9 route up the sideline. Expects the ball.

R: Gets vertical through middle of field. Assures proper spacing. Expects the ball.

L: Gets vertical. Expects the ball.

Z: Gets wide split to stretch free safety. Runs a 9 route up the sideline. Expects the ball.

It is fun to shift to this formation and play on first down because the five-wide receiver set gives the defense five different receivers to defend when they could possibly be in a run-stopping defensive alignment. The defense may rush one more defender than the offense has blockers, which is why you back the quarterback two yards deeper than normal so he can deliver the ball before an outside rusher can get to him. It is rare that this happens, but do it just in case. Tell the quarterback to get a good pre-snap read and make a quick decision who to throw it to. Drill the quarterback to release the ball quickly, and don't take a sack. Make a decision, and throw! If you don't complete the pass, it is no big deal. You have more downs.

Pass When They Are Expecting Run

As an offensive coach, you would obviously like to throw the ball when the defense is expecting the run. The key is to know when to do this. For some reason, most defensive coaches anticipate run on first down. This down is a perfect time to fake the run, entice the defense to overreact, and get one of your receivers open. This tactic is more effective when you have a defender who doesn't play with his eyes or overplays the run, failing to execute his pass assignment.

Take Advantage of Overaggressive, Undisciplined Defenders

Find the defensive player who tries to do more than he is asked or supposed to do. Once you have identified that defender, show him a run-action that will get him to bite while sending a receiver on a bomb. Find the safety or corner who has his eyes on the running backs and the quarterback rather than his line key. This defender is susceptible to deceptive actions in the backfield. By the time he realizes the running back doesn't have the ball, your receiver has blown by him. The one or two steps that the defender takes to stop your run-action will be all the time needed to get your receiver past a deep defender. This is your way of exploiting an undisciplined defensive back and going for the bomb or taking advantage of an overly aggressive linebacker and picking up the yardage necessary for a pivotal first down. A perfect example is the fourth-and-short situation late in the game when the offensive team lines up in a typical run formation, then fakes a run and throws to an absolutely wide-open receiver.

"A team should never practice on a field that is not lined. Your players have to become aware of the field's boundaries."

—John Madden

Wide Receiver Splits and Landmarks

ESPN Top 10 Dilemma

You are watching ESPN top 10 highlights one night, and there it appears: the play from heaven. That bunch formation, two-point play versus bracket coverage you've been looking long and hard for. You rewind, play, pause, rewind, play, pause until you memorize that beautiful symphony of movement that results in a wide-open receiver catching the ball for the winning two points. You are sure this is the play that will make the difference in next year's quest for the championship! If you run the same route versus the same defense it should work, right? *Wrong!*

Rewind and Pay Attention: Routes With Purpose

The more you play, pause, and rewind, you begin to notice little things such as how all of the wide receivers seemed to pay special attention to how and where they initially lined up. On the snap of the ball, each receiver departed the line in an almost staggered fashion, which aided in their releases. They all ran routes at very different yet specific depths that resulted in one of them left uncovered. You notice that every wide receiver in the route celebrated as if they had caught the winning pass. They act as though their teammate caught the pass because they did their part to make it happen. The routes were run with purpose with each player knowing the importance of his role in the play. Yes, the route combination is ingenious, but as the saying goes, "The difference is in the details."

Be careful when you discover a great play on ESPN that you analyze the small details that contributed to the success of the play. If when implementing the play you pay attention to just the routes and formation, you will not get the results you expect.

This chapter will look at the use of landmarks and how they help to line up in the optimal position for success of the play. Landmarks are yard lines, hash marks, numbers, goalposts, and any other point of reference utilized to help the wide receiver line up in the optimal pre-snap position necessary for the success of the play. Giving your players specific landmarks for specific plays is one of the little things that turns into a big thing. Landmarks are used to maximize defensive stretch based on the position of the ball on the field and the routes being run. Different landmarks are used for different plays. Spacing is the key to stretching the defense, and landmarks are the tools used to ensure, not guess, where to line up.

It is interesting to watch opposing teams try to emulate our SNH attack here at Carmel High School. We were one of the first high schools in this area to run a fast and efficient SNH system. As years pass, we have seen teams borrow many of our plays and/or formations. It resembles our offense at times, but what becomes evident is a lack of attention to details. Without sufficient attention spent on the extremely important details of the play, they look similar, but the execution just isn't there.

To execute an effective SNH balanced attack, certain things need to take place. Nothing can ruin good X's and O's better than a poor stance, eyes, alignment, takeoff, assignment, precision of route, depth of route, catching football, and so forth. It matters that your receivers line up in specific spots and run disciplined routes while your quarterback is executing the proper footwork necessary to be in sync. Details matter! They matter at every position.

The reasons that one team executes better than the other lie on the practice field. One team has every position group coaching and teaching the specific details that make a play work, while the other team depends on the X's and O's (scheme) for success.

"For the play to work, you must work the play."

—Patty "Cakes" Johnston

Let the Players Know Their Purpose/Role

Do your wide receivers know *why* they are doing what they are doing? As a coach, you must make it very clear not only what they are to do on any given play, but also how that contributes to the overall success of the play. Any help that you can give your players beyond the actual name and assignment can be the difference in its success. If you are going to implement a supercharged SNH attack, you must be willing to put in the time to do the homework necessary to equip your players with not only high-quality X's and O's, but high-quality skill development and teaching.

When you tell the player what his purpose/role is in the play and how it contributes to its success, it is more meaningful to the player and in turn you get a better effort and more attention to detail. If a player knows why his route is relevant to the play, then he is more apt to execute it with purpose and urgency. If he knows the play will not work unless he does his job, he is more likely to make sure he gets it done. Once you have not only explained to the player his assignment, but also how crucial it is to the overall success of the play, he will become much more aware of the little things like finding his landmarks before executing his actual route.

Only One Guy Will Get The Rock

The SNH system could have as many as five wide receivers that participate in any given play, but only one of them will get "the rock." The pass is completed to one receiver, but it is the other four guys in the route that make it happen. One of the wide receivers might have threatened a zone, stretching a defender enough to get a good window for the quarterback, or maybe it is a wide receiver that rubs a defensive back just long enough to get his teammate open. This stuff doesn't happen on SNH teams that depend on great X's and O's to make a great passing game. X's and O's are obviously important, but it isn't until you get a group of wide receivers that are attentive to detail and are willing to play for each other that you supercharge your SNH attack. Remind your wide receivers from the first day of spring practice that it is a long season. They will have games, practices, scrimmages, passing leagues that, for whatever reason, they catch a bunch of passes, and others where they may not have any catches at all. Start from day one telling your wide receivers, "We play with only one ball. Do your job, expect the ball, but the quarterback is going to read the defense and throw to the open receiver, whether that is you or not. Enjoy and share the success of your teammate. Feel just as good helping your buddy get open as it is to make the catch yourself." The four wide receivers in total make or break every play. Every play is designed in such a way that, if every wide receiver does his job, the play will work.

Execution Is No Accident

When you watch a supercharged SNH attack in action, you will notice wide receivers turned wide open or more than one receiver open on any given play. This execution is no accident! This result occurs when the following take place:

- You get a group of players who properly train and condition in the off-season while their coach seeks out help and advice as to improve and/or tweak their SNH attack.
- When spring arrives, the head coach presents anything new in a detailed, organized, multi-modality fashion that meets the learning needs of all of his players. Any new plays and old plays are dissected into every detail that makes a play work. The coach uses spring practice to allocate the time necessary to introduce concepts and assignments without having to worry about an opponent that weekend. He breaks down everything from stance, alignment, assignment, and purpose of play into very coachable parts. This stage is the time to be very detailed and assignment-oriented.

- Summer comes, and the coach has his entire summer mapped out. Weight training, passing leagues, scrimmages, and such are organized so everyone knows what the summer commitment is. Summer is chaotic with players doing all sorts of things that bite into the time you have with them. You won't have time during your regular season to cover all of the small details that contribute to the success of a play due to the fact that you have an opponent to play, and time needs to be spent planning and perfecting a plan of attack.

Time Well Spent

You have failed your players if you are not specific about where and why they line up where they do. It is up to you to not implement a pass route unless you know the *where* and *why* of every player that is on the field. If it means implementing less and focusing more on getting good at the boring details, then so be it. It doesn't take much to mess up a play even when most of the team is doing what they are supposed to do. By paying attention to the details of a play and then empowering your player by imparting that knowledge to him, you give him personally and your team collectively a chance to get the absolute most out of that play. Even if the play is a flop, you can rest easy knowing your players were in the alignment most appropriate for its success. This applies to both the run and pass game. See that your players don't take splits haphazardly. Give them a reason to line up where they do every play. Do this, and you will surely supercharge your SNH.

Same Plays, Different Results

When two similar teams run the same pass play against the same defense, and one team executes smoothly while the second stumbles all over themselves, it is because one coach drew it up on a board and told the team to run it, while a different coach researched deeply based on what defenses he must defeat to win the championship. He spent valuable time to ensure that he appealed to all the various learning modes of his players by talking, walking, showing video, drawing it on a board, and lastly having the players teach it to a group of lower-level players. During a walk-through or alignment period, the coach physically stood next to his player while in formation and explained to him exactly where he is to line up, where he is going, and why. From that point, mistakes made by the player are corrected by the coach. Mistakes must be discovered at practice, not in the game. As long as coaching/teaching has taken place, the coach can hold the player accountable.

Both teams may be in the same formation, but this is where the similarities end. If you examine closely both trips formations, they will look noticeably different. The team that struggles will probably have all three of the wide receivers equally spaced. This is not to say that equal spacing is a bad thing. It may be appropriate for a couple of plays in the playbook, but numerous pass plays out of trips formation require unequal spacing between wide receivers. Teams that don't know how to coach a sophisticated passing game will pound their heads against a wall wondering why when they run that play they discovered at a clinic or borrowed from an opponent doesn't work. Without proper alignment and spacing that is facilitated by use of landmarks, the struggling team may be running the same pass routes, but nothing else. Because of their alignment, stance, spacing, and so forth, the play is not being run to its potential. There are no throwing windows or open receivers because the wide receivers are either too close together, too far apart, or lined up too deep in the backfield to effectively attack vertically. They are the same plays against the same defenses. Why does one team execute more efficiently than the other? The answer is in the details. The more successful team does the following:

- *Has wide receivers physically prepared to get off the line of scrimmage.* In other words, they are aligned appropriately in an athletic stance, with the front foot up, eyes up, shoulders over knees, and legs like springs just prior to the snap. They roll over the front foot on takeoff, take no false steps, pound the hammer, keep the shoulders over knees in breaks, stem, get on the defender's hip, look the ball into the dimples, and so forth. They do all of this while knowing what purpose they serve in the play. They explode off the line knowing that they can always throttle down later in the route.

  Some routes do require that one receiver release slower than another or pause and creep into a route, then accelerate. Generally speaking, however, you want your wide receivers to be as close to the line of scrimmage as possible in a springy two-point sprinter's stance, ready to explode and attack vertically. The intention is to attack aggressively, forcing the defense to either attach to and guard a wide receiver man-to-man or drop into a zone as quickly as possible. This quickly gets the receivers to where they should be to give the quarterback a clean, fast read on the defenders.

- *Uses the natural markings on the field (hash, numbers, yard lines, goal post, etc.) to space themselves in a way that facilitates the proper horizontal and/or vertical stretch necessary for the play.* At the high school level, the field is broken into three equal parts. When you are on a hash (which, when you analyze it, you are most of the time), you have two-thirds of the field to work with. You must also keep in mind the arm strength of your quarterback when assigning splits to your wide receivers. There may be instances when you eliminate a play from the playbook because the play may necessitate a split or throw that is beyond the quarterback's capabilities. This is a fine line sometimes, and you must be sensitive to it.

- *Runs routes at the precise depth and speed.* That is, 13 yards means 13 yards, not 12 1/2 or 13 1/2. The only way you can ensure the proper stretch of the defense and timing with the quarterback is to be a fanatic about the proper depth of routes. When the wide receiver who is supposed to run a 13-yard out runs a 10-yard out and the wide receiver who is supposed to run a three-yard out runs a five-yard out, chaos will ensue (Figure 16-1). This simple lack of detail is what allows the strong safety to cover two receivers at the same time. If those wide receivers had run their routes at the correct depth quickly, they would have forced the strong safety to cover one receiver, leaving the other one open (Figure 16-2). Pay attention to the details in order to supercharge your SNH system, or any system for that matter.

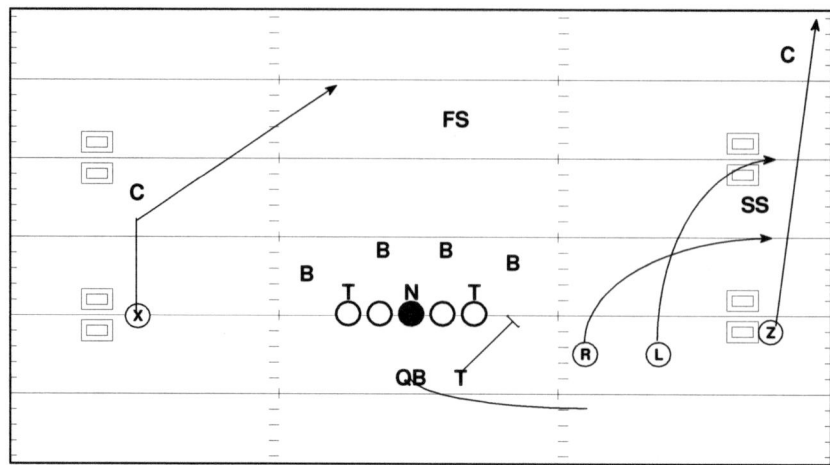

Figure 16-1. Flood with bad routes—strong safety able to cover two guys

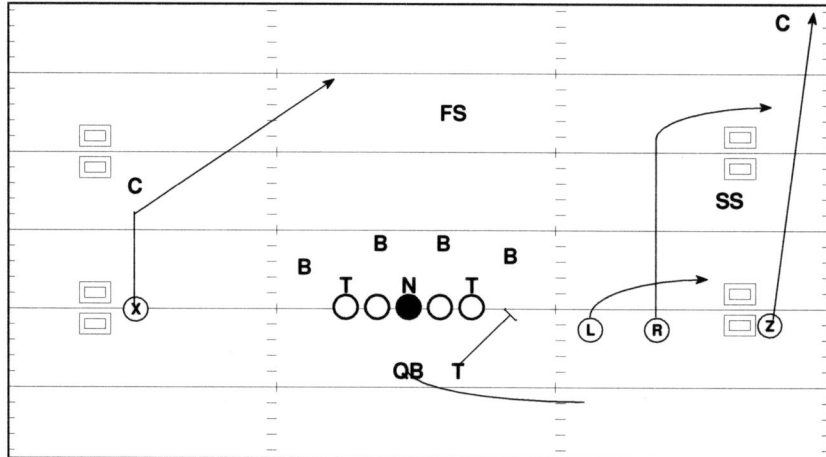

Figure 16-2. Flood with good routes—strong safety not able to cover two guys

Spread 'Em Out Wisely

Don't forget the actual name of your offense is *spread no-huddle*. Spread 'em out, but spread them with reason and purpose. Spread them out wisely. Proper spacing and alignment are necessary to stretch the defensive secondary in the passing game and get defenders out of the box in the running game. Use landmarks on the field to determine wide receiver splits. Spread the defense maximally horizontally and vertically when facing typical zone defenses, and bring your splits in against man coverage when utilizing rub or crossing routes. You would be amazed at what defenders will do to exaggerated splits and/or tight alignments. You may find that you are able to displace or stretch numerous defenders at a time merely by placing wide receivers at strategically placed splits and depths. Between your emphasis on spacing and precise distance on their routes, the wide receivers will thrive, and you can feel good as a coach that you put your players in a position to be successful.

Wide Receiver Splits Help the Pass Game

Insist that your wide receivers align correctly for every pass and run. If the ball is on the hash or close to it (which it is about 80 percent of the time), you have a full two-thirds of the field to spread the secondary out and execute routes. There is not much room into the sideline, but look at the positive side of the situation and take advantage of what is given to you. It would be impossible to give you every rule for every play. It is up to you to analyze the purpose or objective of the play and make sure your wide receivers are in the optimal spot to achieve their objective.

Receivers can use the line of scrimmage, hash marks, numbers, goal-posts, and any other incidental landmarks that can help your wide receivers line up in the spots necessary for the play to work. An effective pass game must take into account proper spacing between your receivers, or they will be running great routes but not be stretching the defense enough to be open. Line your wide receivers up so that, based on their spacing and depth of their routes, they will entice the defense to execute their assignment, thus opening and widening windows to throw in.

Hug the Line of Scrimmage

Wide receivers should hug the line of scrimmage as much as possible to get vertical into the secondary and threaten defenders. A good stance that crowds the line of scrimmage helps the wide receiver to get vertical immediately. It is easier for the quarterback to make his read because the defense is now forced to react quickly to a vertical offensive threat. The quarterback can now make his decision about who to throw to quicker, thus decreasing the amount of time the offensive line must block. Not only must spacing between wide receivers be correct, you must make also make sure that your wide receivers that are supposed to be off the ball hug the line of scrimmage as much as possible unless being deep in the backfield is necessary for proper timing of the play. It should not take your wide receiver three steps just to get to the line of scrimmage because he's lined up too deep. Your quarterback is counting on his wide receivers to be certain places, executing certain routes. In order for the quarterback to get a fast, clean read, he needs his wide receivers downfield, attacking the defense so he can read how the defense is reacting. If it takes too long for the wide receiver to get downfield because he is lined up too deep in the backfield, the quarterback's read is slower, and thus more difficult.

Wide Receiver Splits Help the Run Game

Wide receiver splits are important in the running as well as the passing game. Anything a wide receiver can do get a defender farther away from where the ball is going or get a better angle on a block is a good thing. Displacing defenders in the running game can only be achieved through a thorough understanding of the purpose and direction of the play and what a wide receiver can do to use landmarks to displace defenders or improve blocking angles. You will have times that wide receivers use the markings on the field to determine their splits and then there are times where their split is predicated on the specific formation or getting to or displacing a specific defender (Figure 16-3). The displaced defender is a square.

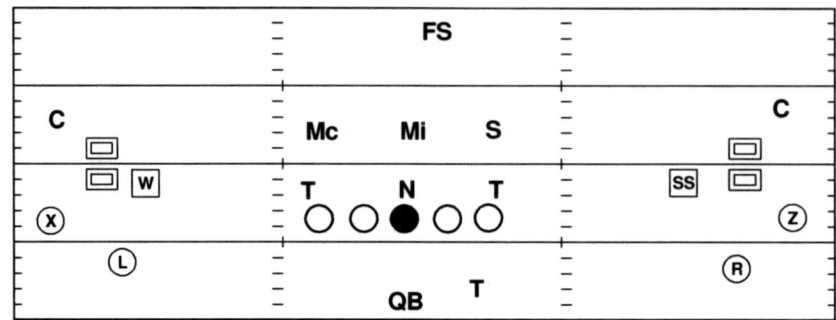

Figure 16-3. Wide splits to displace a defender—run game (Ken)

Alignment Period: No Lineman Required

You might want to consider devoting an entire period of practice to proper wide receiver alignments. You don't need the entire team, just quarterbacks, running backs, tight ends, and wide receivers. It may be the best five to eight minutes you spend during your offensive practice. The perfect sequence of events would be as follows:

• Present the play in its entirety in a meeting or walk-through. Utilize a venue where the coach can relate not only the X's and O's of the play, but all of the nuances that contribute to the success of the play. Cover the splits and alignments necessary to stretch the defense appropriately.

• Once the player has digested this information in the meeting, then follow up during practice with an alignment period in which he is instructed where to physically line up for the play to work. This period is a great opportunity to fine-tune your signaling and alignment. You don't need to run the play! Get the signal to your players, and have them quickly align for optimum execution of the play. Get a signal to the wide receivers, and make sure their alignment is correct for every route you plan on running in the game.

The wide receivers should have a reason for lining up where they do. Trips formation with three wide receivers lined up to one side will be different for every play. Three receivers may be split to the wide field, but how and where they are lined up is predicated on the purpose of the play. Cover all the logistics of the play during meeting time so you can run your alignment drill in rapid-fire fashion. This period is good to incorporate any shifts or motions that will be utilized. Even if you have to lengthen the period a short amount, this is time well spent.

Be Ready for the Team Period

You do not want to get to a team period and have to be coaching shifts, motions, and splits. You want reps and rhythm when you get to your team period. The last thing your offensive coordinator wants during team period is his wide receiver coach taking up valuable time telling his players where to line up. Not only do the wide receivers know where to line up, they should get in a stance that will allow them to take off quickly, getting vertical in their route and threatening defenders. Try to get the alignment details done in a controlled period where everyone leaves the period knowing where they line up. When the team period comes, they know exactly where to go and what to do. The entire offensive team period will flow more smoothly.

Use Anything That Makes Sense to Your Players

One day at practice, we were implementing a new play. The play required one of our wide receivers to cross the field at a specific angle. The player who was running this route asked me what angle he should take across the field. I pointed and told him to "Run at that gate." The gate was a gate allowing entrance to the stadium. From that point on, we used the gate at the end of our football field as a point of reference and destination point for our wide receiver to run. If we were playing at an opponent's field, we would visualize the gate. After executing the play successfully, I asked the players what name to give the play. Their response was: "Let's call it 'gate.'" We quickly and collectively came up with a sideline signal for gate, and viola, a play was born! We normally give routes one-word descriptions so all wide receivers must memorize their assignment. It takes repetition, but your players will grasp it. The possibilities are endless!

"Regard your soldiers as children, and they may follow you wherever you may lead. Look upon them as beloved sons and they will stand by you unto death."

—Sun Tzu

Spread No-Huddle Dropback Pass Plays

This chapter includes the following plays:
- Bunch 70 Irish
- Bunch 70 Over
- Pat 70 Divide
- Right 70 Mesh
- Bronco
- Left 70 Smash

Bunch 70 Irish

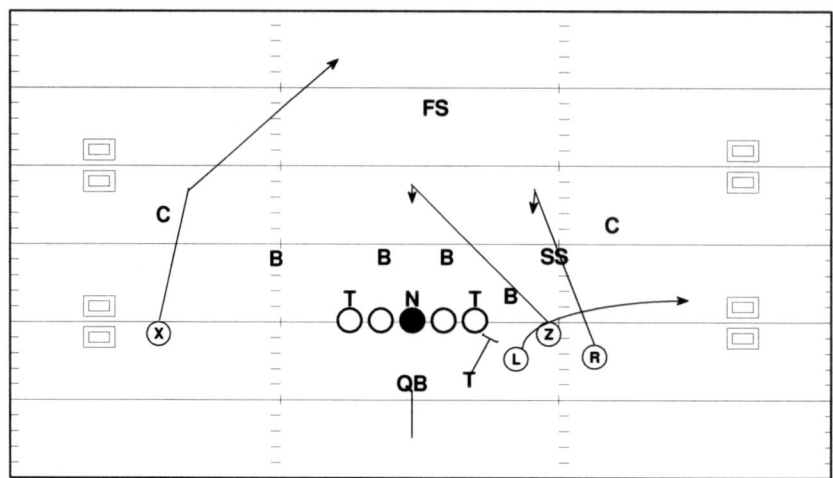

Figure 17-1

Assignments:

Q: Checks rush to playside. Gets to six-yard depth on sprint. Three steps in 70. Knows down-and-distance. Hits L quickly if open. Eyes go inside from Z to R.

T: Aggressive block on outside linebacker. Works head outside in sprint. If no rush, looks to help inside and back.

X: Backside post. Runs hard to set up backside post and corner.

Z: Must avoid reroute! Gets to eight yards over center. Sits and gets numbers to quarterback.

L: Runs straight to flat.

R: Avoids reroute. Gets to six yards where Z initially lined up. Sits, gets numbers to the quarterback.

Notes:
- Bunch 70 Irish is a basic route that is functional against man, zone, or bracket.
- This is a good third-and-four to -seven possession route.
- Motion or shift L, R, and T into their positions shown in Figure 17-1 to gain leverage.
- L to the flat opens up quick sometimes for an easy first down on third-and-short.
- Versus a four-man rush, motion T wide to the bunch side to get defensive backs out of the box.
- You can tag any route to give you tremendous flexibility to get first down.
- Inside wide receivers play "basketball." Use body to get open. Quarterback throws where necessary.

Bunch 70 Over

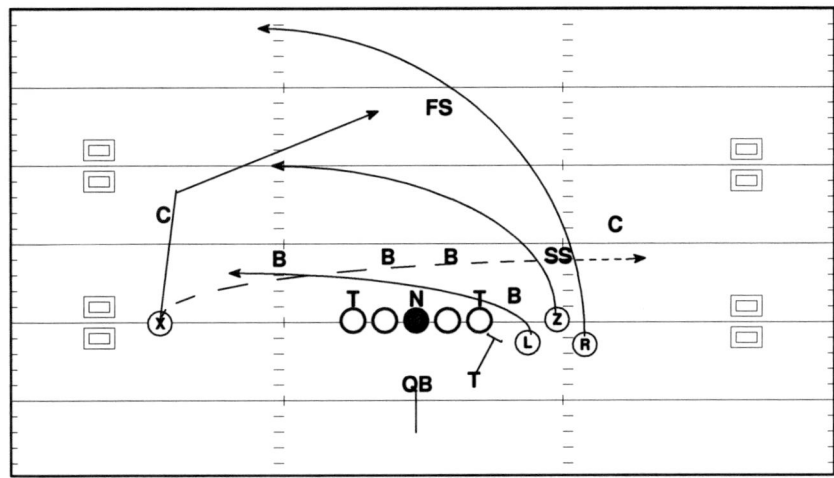

Figure 17-2

Assignments:

Q: Checks rush from outside. Five-step drop reading undercover. Looks to X on drag versus man.

T: Aggressive block on outside linebacker. Works eyes inside if no rush. Looks to inside linebacker if fan call.

X: Backside post. If X drag is tagged, then avoids reroute and gets across field no more than three yards with path of least resistance.

Z: Must avoid reroute! Gets to 10 yards, and stays straight across to sideline.

L: No vertical. Drags across at no more than three yards depth. Avoids reroute!

R: Hard vertical to six yards, then breaks over the top and crosses the field.

Notes:
- Bunch 70 Over is a great change-up bunch play that gets wide receivers to opposite field.
- Give wide receivers great rubs while allowing them to run away from slower defenders.
- Tag R with a corner route for a different stretch.
- Tag R with a China route for short yardage.
- Quarterback must use deeper drop utilizing good footwork to allow routes to develop.
- T flat is a good two-point play versus man coverage.

Pat 70 Divide

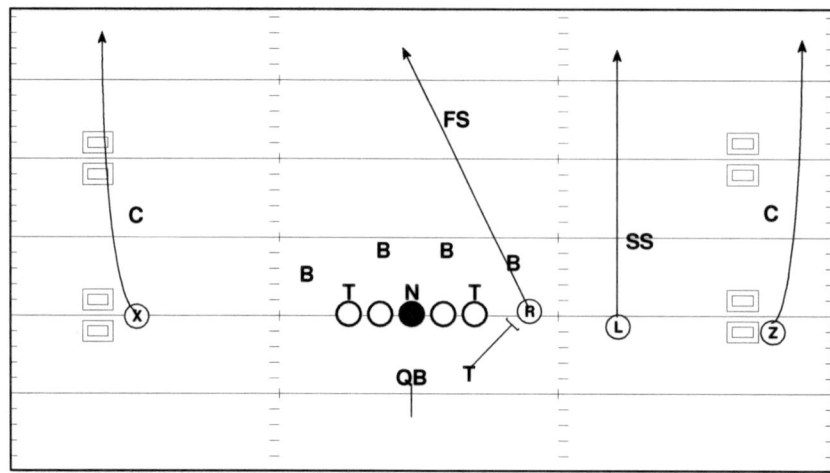

Figure 17-3

Assignments:

Q: Three-step drop. Reads free safety. Throws to R or L versus cover 3, and L or Z versus cover 2.

T: 70 protection. Eyes go from outside to inside. Eyes on inside linebacker if fan call.

X: 9 route on sideline to stretch free safety. Anticipates ball thrown to him.

R: Gets vertical ASAP, attacking opposite shoulder of free safety. Avoids reroute!

L: Hard vertical attacking outside shoulder of #2 defender. Avoids reroute. Finds window between free safety and #2 defender. Must keep width to avoid free safety and under coverage.

Z: 9 route on sideline to stretch free safety. Anticipates ball thrown to him.

Notes:
- Pat 70 Divide is a great way to attack three-deep secondary.
- Play accomplishes "all vertical" principles out of trips formation.
- Pass can be thrown quickly between strong safety and free safety or deep.
- Potential mismatch between L and strong safety in quarters coverage.
- Tag X or Z with a dig route ounce deep threat is established.
- Tag T flat if four-man rush.

Right 70 Mesh

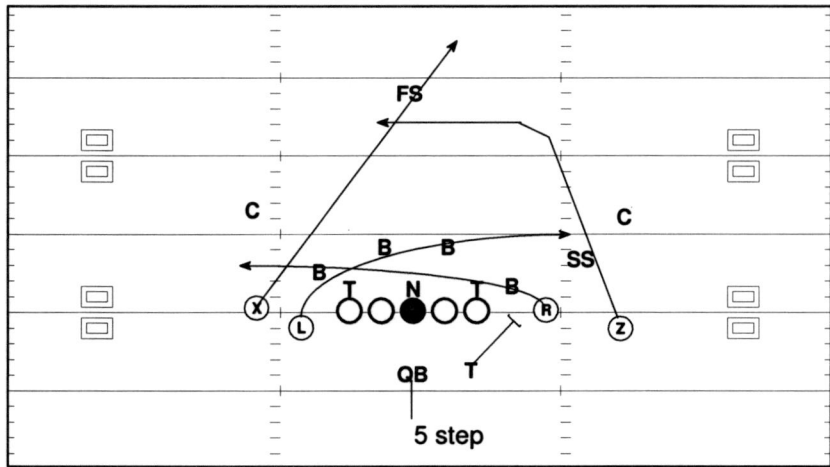

Figure 17-4

Assignments:

Q: Five-step drop. Reads free safety while feeling undercover. Throws to X if free safety bites. Throws to Z if free safety gets deep middle. Thinks draggers versus man cover or comes wide open.

T: Aggressive block on outside linebacker. Works head outside. If no rush, looks to help inside and back.

X: Gets tight split. Gets vertical ASAP running through free safety.

R: Drag route. Avoids reroute. Gets to three yards depth at opposite tackle.

L: Drag route. Avoids reroute. Gets to five yards depth at opposite tackle.

Z: Vertical to 13 yards. Dig route. No deeper than 13 yards. Finds window between inside linebackers.

Notes:
- 70 Mesh is a great stretch route versus one free safety.
- Rub between L and R to help wide receivers run away from defensive backs in man coverage.
- Opposite flats can be wide open versus man coverage.

Bronco

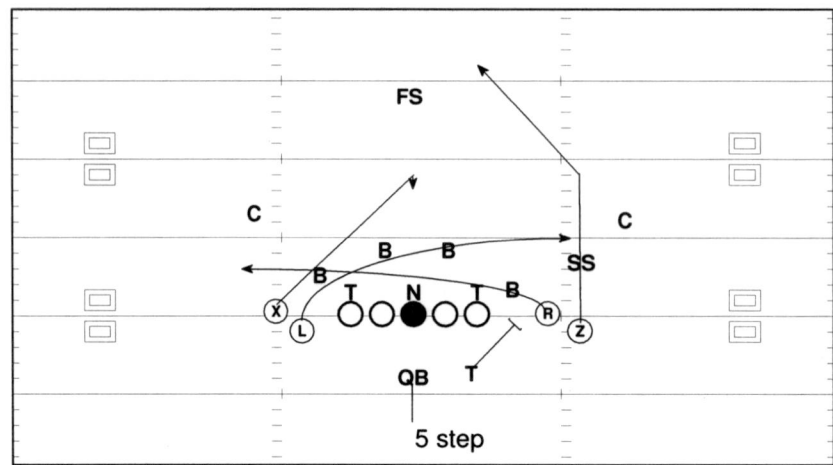

Figure 17-5

Assignments:

Q: Five-step drop. Reads free safety while feeling undercover. Reads inside linebacker to X side. Looks dragger to X sitting over center.

T: Aggressive block on outside linebacker. Works head outside. If no rush, looks to help inside and back.

X: Gets tight split. Angle route to 8 to 10 yards, sitting over center.

R: Drag route. Avoids reroute. Gets to three yards depth at opposite tackle.

L: Drag route. Avoids reroute. Gets to five yards depth at opposite tackle.

Z: Post route. Route can be tagged for corner route.

Notes:
- Dragging wide receivers open up the middle of the formation.
- Tag T to the flat for extra stretch versus four-man rush.
- Tag Z to the corner for change-up.

Left 70 Smash

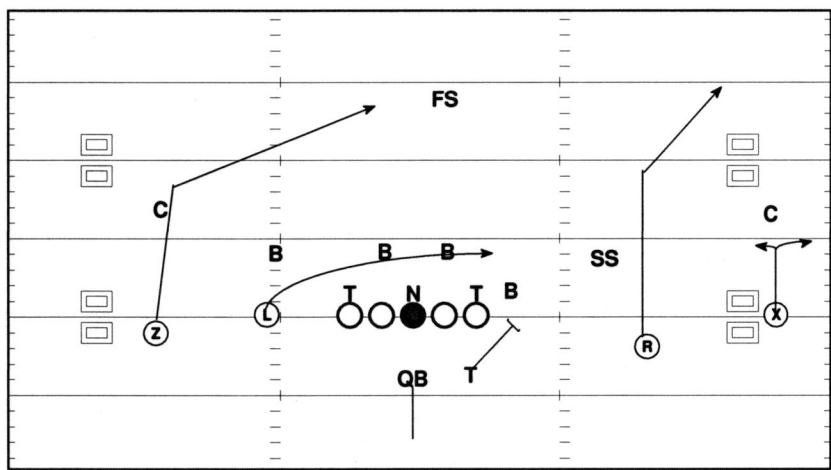

Figure 17-6

Assignments:

Q: Checks rush to playside. Takes comfortable three-step drop. Reads #1 defender (corner). Adjusts drop at any time to throw to X or R.

T: Aggressive block on outside linebacker. Works head outside. If no rush, looks to help inside and back.

X: Three- to five-yard out or in route. Makes himself visible.

L: Drag route. Avoids reroute. Gets to four to five yards depth at opposite tackle.

R: Gets vertical to eight yards, avoiding reroute. Goes to corner, finding window between free safety and corner.

Z: Backside post.

Notes:
- Smash is an age-old way of attacking a three-deep secondary.
- X and Z can be creative in the way they influence the corner.
- Play is a great route versus quarters coverage as well.
- Play is a simple read for a young quarterback: one man, the corner.
- R must find soft spot between corner and safety.

"You can't stop at every dog that barks, or you'll never get the mail delivered."

—Phog Allen

Spread No-Huddle Sprint Pass Plays

This chapter includes the following plays:
- Left 60 Coffee
- Left 60 Smash
- Left 60 Trail
- Right 69 Tags
- Pat 50 Choice
- Pat 60 Angle
- Trips 60 Flood
- Trips 60 Flood Switch
- Pat 60 Stops
- Trips 60 Trail
- Pat 60 Trash
- Bunch 60 Flood
- Bunch 60 Ladder

Left 60 Coffee

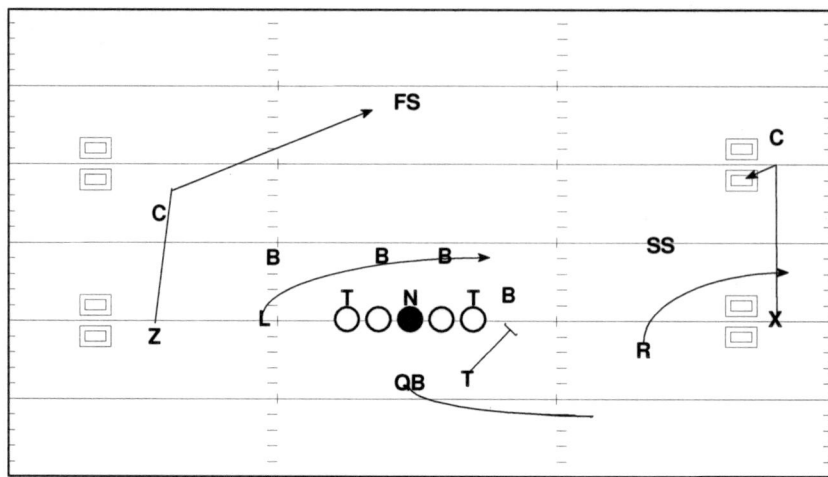

Figure 18-1

Assignments:

Q: Checks rush to playside. Gets to six-yard depth on sprint. Reads #2 defender.

T: Aggressive block on outside linebacker. Works head outside. If no rush, looks to help inside and back.

X: Runs a 10-yard stop route. Shows quarterback numbers. Comes back to quarterback finding window.

L: Drag route. Avoids reroute. Gets to four to five yards depth at opposite tackle.

R: Runs a three-yard flat route. Three yards and straight to sideline.

Z: Backside post route. Runs hard to set up backside post or corner.

Notes:
- Coffee is a simple one-man read curl-flat combo route.
- Sprint helps quarterback vision while one-man read focuses attention.
- R must get to flat quickly to aid quick decision by quarterback.
- Execute wheel route by R versus aggressive corner.
- Stop and throw backside post or corner versus aggressive free safety.

Left 60 Smash

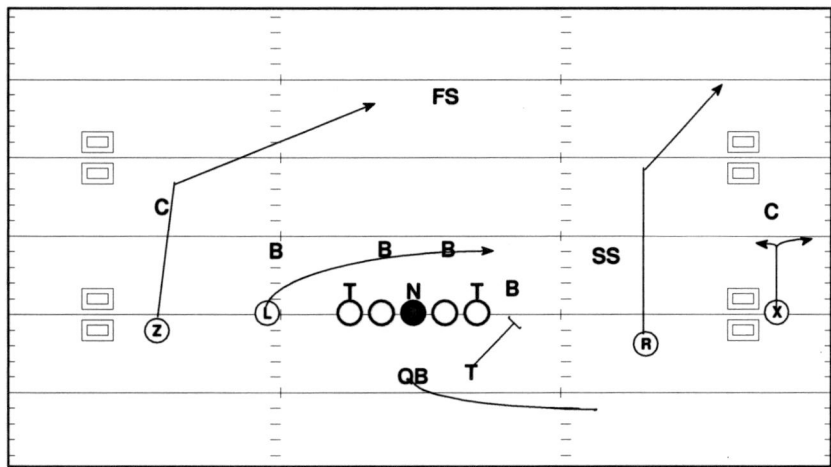

Figure 18-2

Assignments:

Q: Checks rush to playside. Gets to six-yard depth on sprint. Reads #1 defender (corner).

T: Aggressive block on outside linebacker. Works head outside. If no rush, looks to help inside and back.

X: Three- to five-yard out or in route. Makes himself visible.

L: Drag route. Avoids reroute. Gets to four to five yards depth at opposite tackle.

R: Gets vertical to eight yards avoiding reroute. Goes to corner finding window between free safety and corner.

Z: Backside post.

Notes:
- X and Z can be creative in the way they influence the corner.
- Left 60 Smash is a great route versus quarters coverage as well.
- Play is a simple read for young quarterback: one man, the corner.
- R must find soft spot between corner and safety.

Left 60 Trail

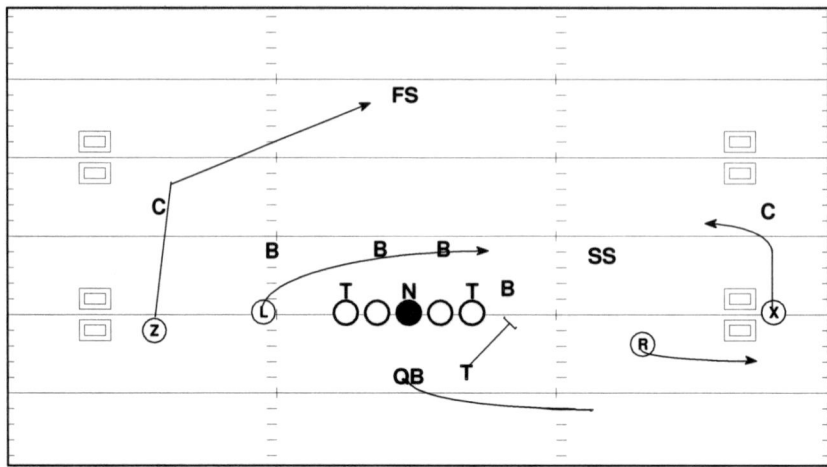

Figure 18-3

Assignments:

Q: Checks rush to playside. Gets to six-yard depth on sprint. Reads #2 defender.

T: Aggressive block on outside linebacker. Works head outside. If no rush, looks to help inside and back.

X: Hard vertical to four to five yards. Hard slant move, then throttles down and finds window.

L: Drag route. Avoids reroute. Gets to four to five yards depth at opposite tackle.

R: Swing route, gets flat, not too deep. Gets eyes to quarterback. Thinks sideline after catch.

Z: Backside post. Runs hard to set up backside post or corner.

Notes:
- Trail is another simple one-man read for quarterback.
- X can vary the depth and speed of his route to best attack the defense.
- Great rub wheel route alternative versus man coverage.
- Sprint stop and tag backside post or corner.

Right 69 Tags

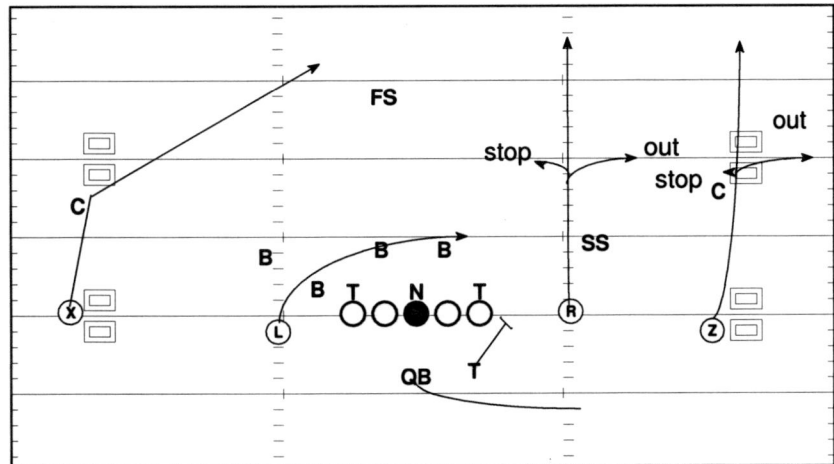

Figure 18-4

Assignments:

Q: Checks rush to playside. Gets to six-yard depth. Looks to tagged receiver.

T: Aggressive block on outside linebacker. Works head outside. If no edge rush, looks inside to help.

X: Backside post route hard to set up backside post or corner. Expects ball.

L: Drag route at five yards at opposite tackle. Avoids reroute.

R: Gets vertical to nearest hash. Speed cut out or stops at 10 yards. Expects ball.

Z: Gets wide split to stretch free safety. Speed cut out or stops at 10 yards. Expects ball.

Notes:
- Look at all the options you have frontside and backside.
- Right 69 Tags is a great possession play.
- Right 69 Tags is a good play versus numerous coverages.
- Right 69 Tags allows you to specifically attack a fish out of water.
- Add China concept to any horizontal stem for change-up.
- Stop quarterback up to make throwback or deep middle passes.
- These routes become option routes with more experienced wide receivers.
- Right 69 Tags is a simple play given to a young quarterback to gain confidence.

Pat 50 Choice

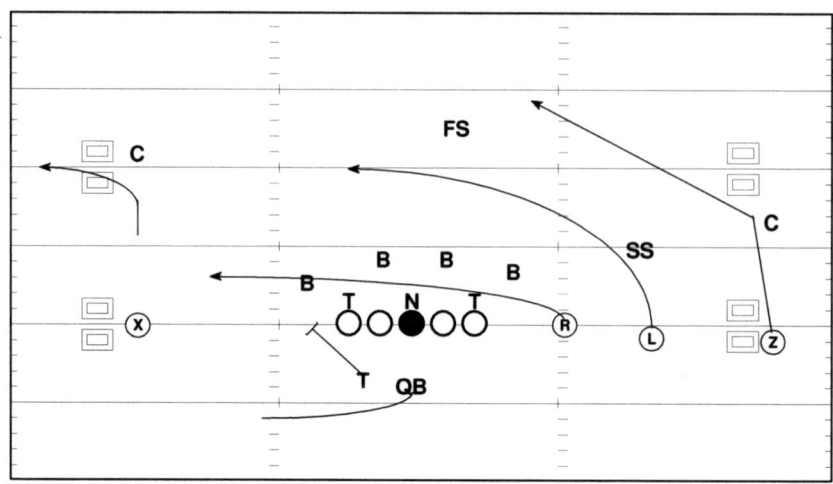

Figure 18-5

Assignments:

Q: Checks rush to playside. Gets to six-yard depth on sprint. Throws out to X, or continues rolling and throws to R dragging.

T: Aggressive block on outside linebacker. Works head outside. If no rush, looks to help inside and back.

X: 10-yard speed cut. Straight to sideline at 10 yards.

R: Shallow drag route. No vertical. Avoids reroute. Three-yard depth at opposite tackle.

L: Drag route. Very little vertical. Must avoid reroute. Gets to 10 yards at opposite tackle.

Z: Backside post. Runs hard to set up backside post or corner.

Notes:
- One-man playside route should become a handoff between quarterback and wide receiver.
- Quarterback can stop roll while backside trips routes can be tagged various ways.
- If X isn't open, then quarterback's eyes can go from hit the dragger to throw it away.
- Show play-action power to trips to hold weakside flat defender.
- Play could potentially become a first down or third-and-seven to -10 play.

Pat 60 Angle

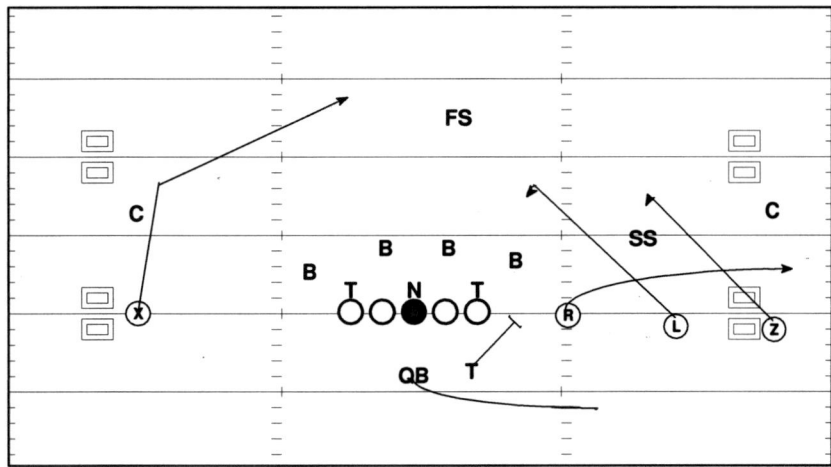

Figure 18-6

Assignments:

Q: Checks rush to playside. Gets to six-yard depth on sprint. Reads #2 defender.

T: Aggressive block on outside linebacker. Works head outside. If no rush, looks to help inside and back.

X: Backside post. Runs hard to set up backside post and corner.

R: Runs straight to flat. No depth.

L: Runs angle route to depth of seven to eight yards, walling off inside linebacker. Turns to quarterback, and shows numbers.

Z: Runs angle route to depth of seven to eight yards, replacing strong safety. Turns to quarterback, and shows numbers.

Notes:
- Angle facilitates good vision and accelerates defensive reaction, which helps read.
- Angled release by wide receivers alternatively threatens defense.
- Numerous tag possibilities threaten defensive weaknesses.
- Switch assignments between trips wide receivers to vary attack.
- Play offers potential wheel route versus lazy safety or overaggressive corner.
- Stop up quarterback, and hit backside post or corner.

Trips 60 Flood

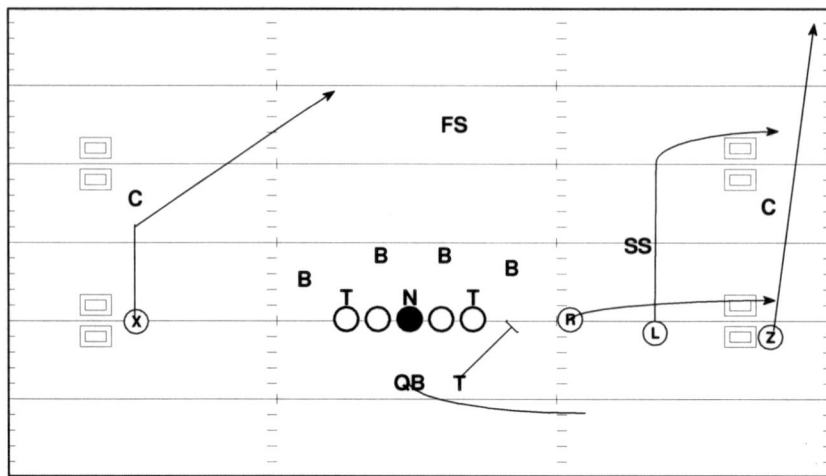

Figure 18-7

Assignments:

Q: Checks rush to playside. Gets to six-yard depth on sprint. Reads #2 defender.

T: Aggressive block on outside linebacker. Works head outside. If no rush, looks to help inside and back.

X: Backside post. Runs hard to set up backside post and corner.

R: Quick flat. No depth necessary. Works straight to sideline.

L: Must get vertical and avoid reroute. Begins speed cut at 10, ends up straight to sideline at 12 yards.

Z: Must get corner to turn back to play while clearing flood area up sideline.

Notes:
- Flood is a basic, but effective, play.
- This versatile play is good versus multiple coverages.
- Hit Z on sideline versus an overaggressive corner.
- Flood is a nice play to give your quarterback good vision while making simple one-man read.
- Tag Z dig when under defenders over flow. Trips 60 Flood is a great third-and-10 to -15 play.
- Get wide split and tag L stop after running this play a few times.
- Flood is a great play to stop up quarterback and throw post versus aggressive free safety.

Trips 60 Flood Switch

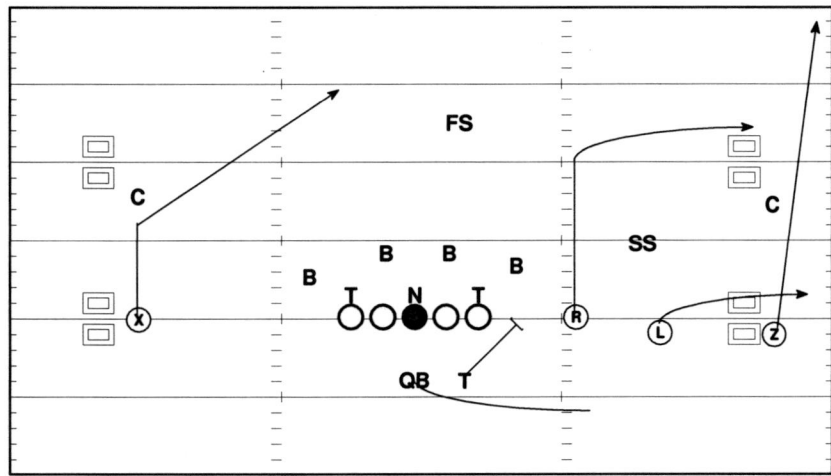

Figure 18-8

Assignments:

Q: Checks rush to playside. Gets to six-yard depth on sprint. Reads #2 defender.

T: Aggressive block on outside linebacker. Works head outside. If no rush, looks to help inside and back.

X: Backside post. Runs hard to set up backside post and corner.

R. Must get vertical and avoid reroute. Begins speed cut at 10, ends up straight to sideline at 12 yards.

L: Quick flat. No depth necessary. Works straight to sideline.

Z: Must get corner to turn back to play while clearing flood area up sideline.

Notes:
- Flood Switch is a basic, but effective play.
- This versatile play is good versus multiple coverages.
- Hit Z on sideline versus an overaggressive corner.
- Flood Switch is a nice play to give your quarterback good vision while making simple one-man read.
- Tag Z dig when under defenders over flow. Flood Switch is a great third-and-10 to -15 play.
- Get wide split and tag L stop after running this play a few times.
- Flood Switch is a great play to stop up quarterback and throw post versus aggressive free safety.

Pat 60 Stops

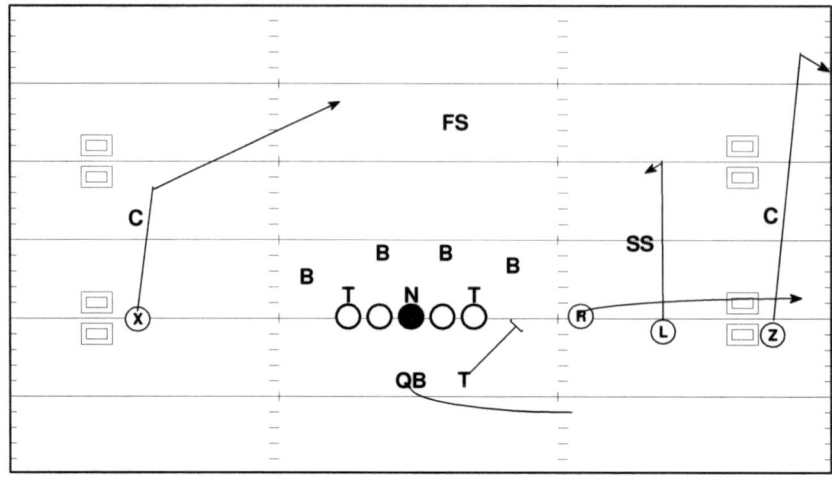

Figure 18-9

Assignments:

Q: Checks rush to playside. Reads #2 defender. Continues roll, throws to Z or out-of-bounds.

T: Aggressive block on outside linebacker. Works head outside. If no rush, looks to help inside and back.

X: Backside post. Runs hard to set up backside post and corner.

R: Quick flat. No depth necessary. Works straight to sideline.

L: 10-yard stop route. Finds window, comes back to quarterback.

Z: 16-yard out. Must be patient and get 16 yards, then comes back to sideline.

Notes:
- This very versatile play is good for third-and-8 to -10 as well as third-and-13 to -16.
- Stops gives quarterback a simple one-man read while having plan B if necessary.
- Quick flat release by R gives quarterback fast, clean read.
- L's split must eliminate inside linebacker flow with sprint.
- Patience by Z getting 15 to 16 yards before coming back to sideline is essential.
- Play offers potential backside tags versus overaggressive free safety.

Trips 60 Trail

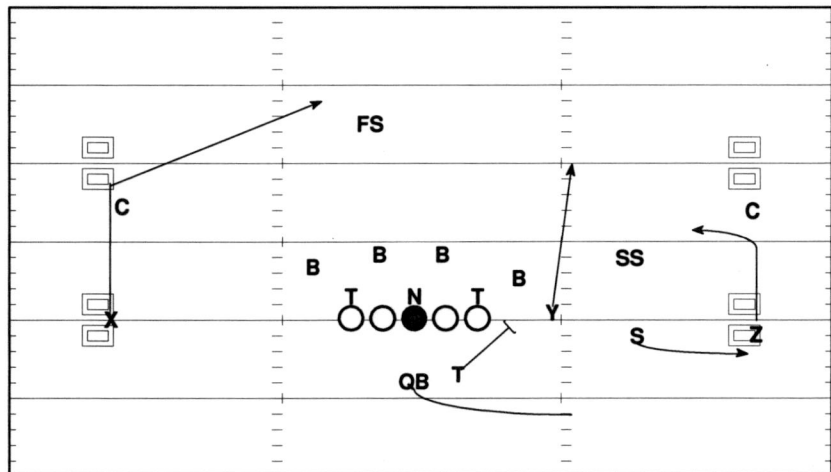

Figure 18-10

Assignments:

Q: Checks rush to playside. Gets to six-yard depth on sprint. Reads #2 defender.

T: Aggressive block on outside linebacker. Works head outside. If no rush, looks to help inside and back.

X: Backside post. Runs hard to set up backside post and corner.

Y: Gets vertical, walling off inside linebacker from curl-flat zone.

S: Swing route, gets flat, not too deep. Gets eyes to quarterback. Thinks sideline after catch.

Z: Hard vertical to four to five yards. Hard slant move, then throttles down and finds window.

Notes:
- Simple second defender read facilitates good vision for quarterback and high percentage throws.
- Splits by S and Z must be wide enough to eliminate under coverage.
- Trail route by S forces strong safety to make quick decision, which helps facilitate fast read by quarterback.
- Trail is a great way to tag S and get the ball to one of your best athletes in space.
- R must rub inside defenders to open windows to perimeter.
- Route is effective versus overaggressive strong safeties.
- Sluggo route by Z versus overaggressive corner is lethal.

Pat 60 Trash

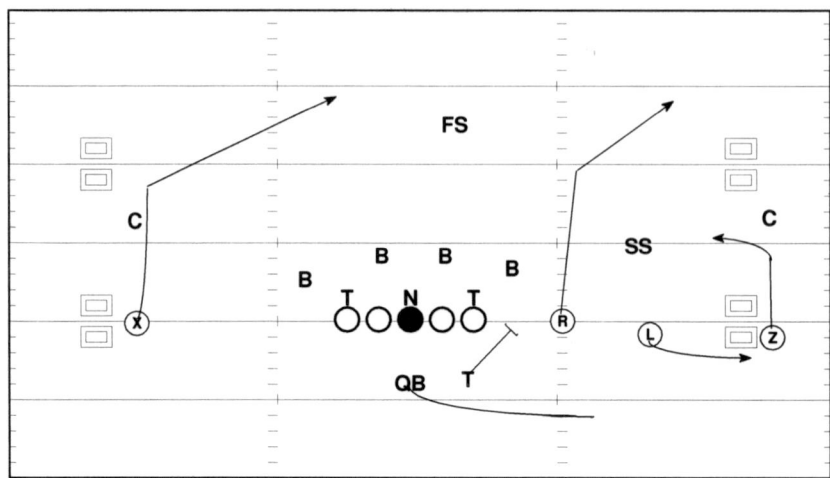

Figure 18-11

Assignments:

Q: Checks rush to playside. Gets to six-yard depth on sprint. Reads #2 defender.

T: Aggressive block on outside linebacker. Works head outside. If no rush, looks to help inside and back.

X: Backside post. Runs hard to set up backside post and corner.

R: Gets vertical. Avoids reroute, then finds window between free safety and corner.

L: Runs trail. Swing route, gets flat, not too deep. Gets eyes to quarterback. Thinks sideline after catch.

Z: Runs trail. Hard vertical to four to five yards. Hard slant move, then throttles down and finds window.

Notes:
- Trash is a nice combo of trail and smash.
- Play is still a simple one-man read for quarterback. Read the play like smash.
- Trash is a great way to stretch the free safety. Stop up sprint, and attack the free safety deep.
- Predetermine throw to L without free safety filling alley.

Bunch 60 Flood

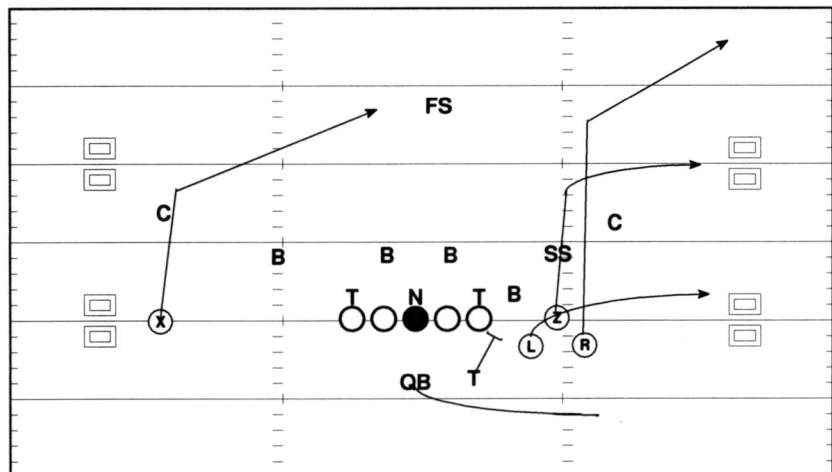

Figure 18-12

Assignments:

Q: Checks rush to playside. Gets to six-yard depth on sprint. Reads #2 defender.

T: Aggressive block on outside linebacker. Works head outside. If no rush, looks to help inside and back.

X: Backside post. Runs hard to set up backside post and corner.

Z: Must avoid reroute! Gets to 10 yards, and breaks straight to sideline.

L: Runs straight to flat.

R: Hard vertical to 12 yards. Goes to corner.

Notes:
- Bunch Flood is a simple multi-level bunch route.
- Bunch formation allows wide receivers plenty of field space to disengage defenders.
- Vertical push by R should clear flat for Z and L.
- Z must not get rerouted vertically. Natural rub between Z and L.
- If Z getting rerouted, then switch routes between L and Z.
- Flood to one side entices free safety to vacate middle of field. Play offers potential throwback.
- Drop back and tag Z drag versus lazy weakside coverage.

Bunch 60 Ladder

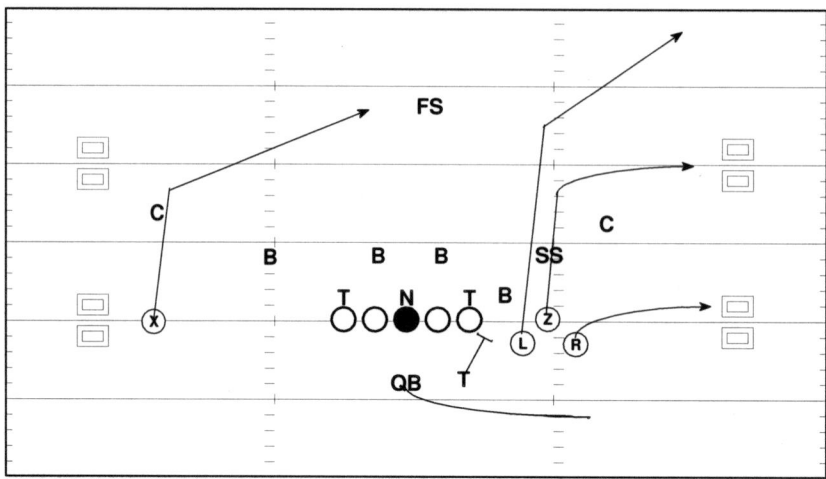

Figure 18-13

Assignments:

Q: Checks rush to playside. Gets to six-yard depth on sprint. Reads #2 defender.

T: Aggressive block on outside linebacker. Works head outside. If no rush, looks to help inside and back.

X: Backside post. Runs hard to set up backside post and corner.

Z: Must avoid reroute! Gets to 10 yards, and breaks straight to sideline.

L: Must avoid reroute! Gets to 12 yards, and goes to corner.

R: Runs straight to flat.

Notes:
- Ladder is a simple multi-level bunch route.
- Bunch formation allows wide receivers plenty of field space to disengage defenders.
- R quickly to flat is good third-and-short play.
- Z must not get rerouted vertically.
- If Z is getting rerouted, then switch routes between L and Z.
- Flood to one side entices free safety to vacate middle of field. Play offers potential throwback.
- Drop back and tag Z drag versus lazy weakside coverage.

Fuse/Thinkstock

"Motivating through fear may work in the short term to get people to do something, but over the long run I believe personal pride is a much greater motivator. It produces far better results that last for a much longer time."

—John Wooden

Spread No-Huddle Run Plays

This chapter includes the following plays:
- Option vs. Even Front
- Option vs. Odd Front
- Trap vs. Even Front
- Trap vs. Odd Front
- Zone vs. Even Front
- Zone vs. Odd Front
- Power vs. Even Front
- Power vs. Odd Front
- Sweep vs. Even Front
- Sweep vs. Odd Front

Option vs. Even Front

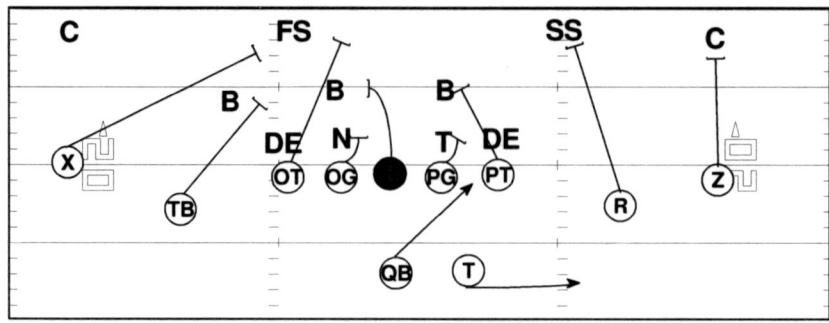

Figure 19-1

Assignments:

PT: Disregards defensive end. Path of least resistance to playside inside linebacker. Gets head to outside and walls inside linebacker.

PG: Reach blocks on defensive tackle. Gets head to playside. Tries to hook or get tie.

C: Takes path to cut off backside inside linebacker. Goes where inside linebacker will be, not where he lines up. Must not let backside inside linebacker cross his face to playside.

OG: Reach blocks on defensive tackle. Gets head to playside. Tries to hook or get tie.

OT: Disregards defensive end. Releases inside. Hits first enemy color, working up to next level. Hits somebody to playside.

Option vs. Odd Front

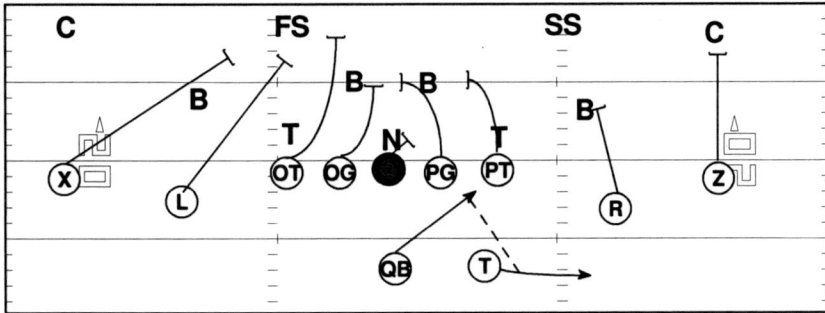

Figure 19-2

Assignments:

PT: Recognizes end man on line of scrimmage. If defensive tackle is end man on line of scrimmage, then path of least resistance to inside linebacker. Gets head to playside. If defensive tackle is not end man on line of scrimmage, then hard reach blocks, trying to hook.

PG: Recognizes depth and angle of backside inside linebacker. Cut him off at the pass. Get head to playside. Wall him off.

C: Reach and hook blocks noseguard. If hook not possible, gets a tie down line of scrimmage.

OG: Gets great angle on backside inside linebacker. If unable to get to him, goes to safety.

OT: Disregards defensive tackle. Gets to third level and finds a safety. Hits somebody downfield.

Trap vs. Even Front

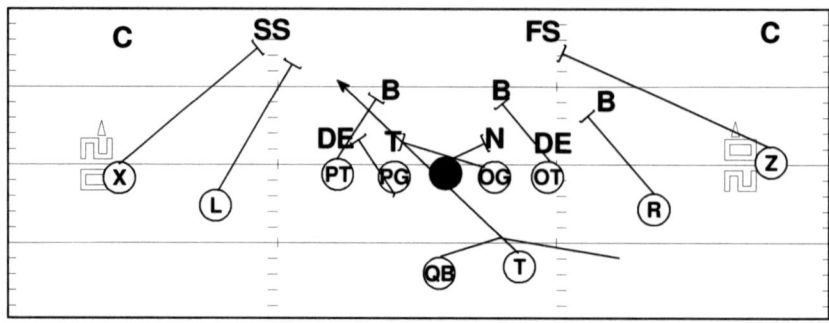

Figure 19-3

Assignments:

PT: Listens for playside guard call. If "me" call, then quick steps inside defensive end and walls off inside on defensive end (gets back to hole). If "you" call, then takes steep angle to playside inside linebacker. Gets head inside, climbs, and walls inside linebacker.

PG: If defensive tackle inside or head up (1 or 2 shade) call "you" telling playside tackle to go to inside linebacker. Quick influence move (pass pro bucket step), then walls defensive end from hole. If defensive tackle is outside shade (3 technique), then calls "me," and goes to playside inside linebacker. Climbs and walls inside linebacker.

C: Blocks back on noseguard. Gets head to playside.

OG: Pulls into line, not backfield. Traps playside defensive tackle with head to inside.

OT: Disregards defensive end. Gets to backside inside linebacker. Climbs and walls.

Trap vs. Odd Front

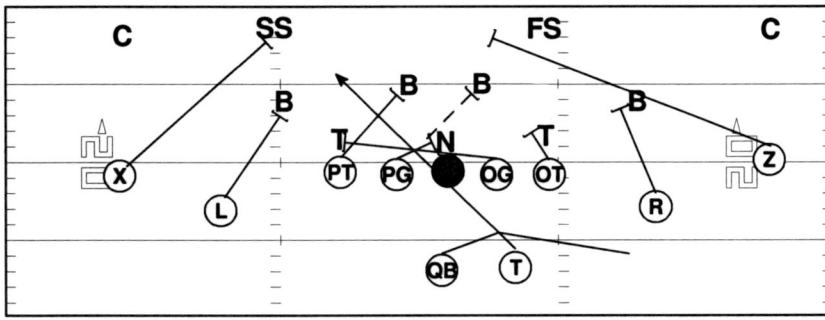

Figure 19-4

Assignments:

PT: Path of least resistance to playside inside linebacker. Anticipates depth and angle of inside linebacker and gets head to playside of inside linebacker. Wall blocks. Running back will be running off his block.

PG: Aggressive double-team with center. Must ensure double-team, then works to backside inside linebacker. Wall blocks backside inside linebacker with head to playside.

C: Aggressive double-team with playside guard. Ensures double-team, and anticipates playside guard coming off on backside inside linebacker. Must blow noseguard into backside inside linebacker.

OG: Pulls into line and traps playside tackle. Gets depth into line, not into backfield. Gets head on inside of defensive tackle. Hits and climbs defensive tackle. Running back will be running off his butt.

OT: Reach steps to playside. Must cut off defensive tackle. If defensive tackle slants outside, then disregards and gets head to playside of inside linebackers.

Zone vs. Even Front

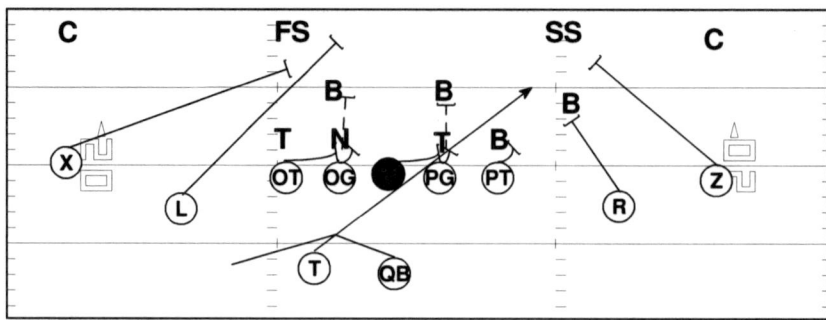

Figure 19-5

Assignments:

PT: Aggressive reach block. If defensive tackle is outside shade, then drives him out. If head-up, then tries to hook working head to outside. Gets at least a tie.

PG: Double-teams defensive tackle with center. Dominates defensive tackle. Comes off to inside linebacker at inside linebacker depth once defensive tackle block is secure. Blocks defensive tackle 1-on-1 if defensive tackle slants strong. Goes directly to inside linebacker if defensive tackle slants weak.

C: Double-teams defensive tackle with playside guard. Dominates defensive tackle. Comes off to inside linebacker at inside linebacker depth once defensive tackle block is secure. Blocks defensive tackle 1-on-1 if defensive tackle slants weak. Goes directly to inside linebacker if defensive tackle slants strong.

OG: Double-teams noseguard with offensive tackle. Dominates noseguard. Comes off to inside linebacker at inside linebacker depth once noseguard block is secure. Blocks noseguard 1-on-1 if defensive tackle slants strong. Goes directly to inside linebacker if inside linebacker slants weak.

OT: Double-teams noseguard with offensive guard. Dominates noseguard. Comes off to inside linebacker at inside linebacker depth once defensive tackle block is secure. Blocks noseguard 1-on-1 if defensive tackle slants weak. Goes directly to inside linebacker if noseguard slants strong.

Zone vs. Odd Front

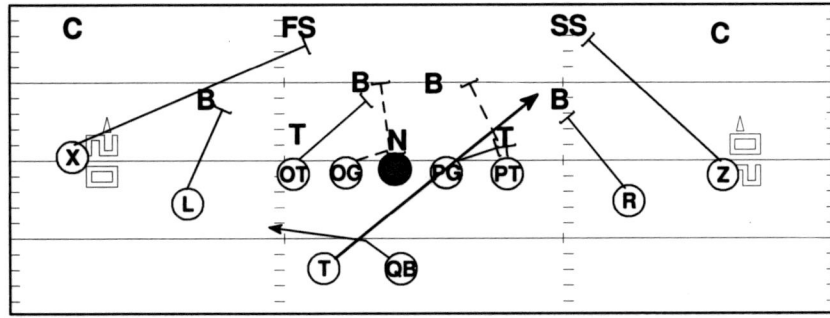

Figure 19-6

Assignments:

PT: Aggressive reach block on defensive tackle. Combo blocks with playside guard. Works to inside linebacker if defensive tackle slants inside. Works to get head outside.

PG: Combo blocks with playside tackle. Works to inside linebacker at linebacker depth. Dominates defensive tackle with eyes on inside linebacker until he gets to inside linebacker depth. Solo blocks on inside linebacker if inside linebacker comes.

C: Aggressive reach on noseguard to playside. Combo blocks with offensive guard. Dominates noseguard. Comes off on backside inside linebacker if noseguard slants weak.

OG: Combo blocks with center. Works to inside linebacker at linebacker depth. Dominates noseguard with eyes on inside linebacker until he gets to inside linebacker depth. Solo blocks on noseguard if noseguard slants weak.

OT: Hard angle to inside linebacker. Tries to get head to playside of inside linebacker.

Power vs. Even Front

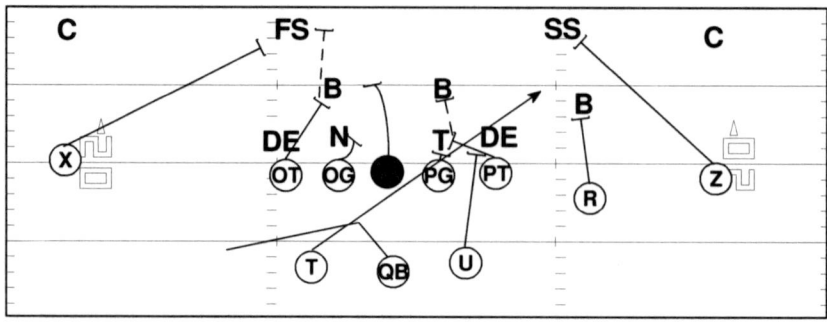

Figure 19-7

Assignments:

PT: Double-team blocks with playside guard on defensive tackle. Secures double-team, then works up to inside linebacker at linebacker level. Dominates defensive tackle before working to inside linebacker.

PG: Double-team blocks with playside tackle on defensive tackle. Drives defensive tackle into backside inside linebacker. Must be ready for playside tackle to release to playside inside linebacker.

C: Takes proper angle to backside inside linebacker. Cuts him off at the pass. Takes angle to where backside inside linebacker will be not where he initially lines up. Must cut off flow of backside inside linebacker.

OG: Reach and hook blocks noseguard. Gets head to playside. Gets at least a tie if he can't hook.

OT: Disregards defensive end, and gets to next level. If he can't get backside inside linebacker, then works up to safety level and hits someone.

U: Inside path to defensive end. Gets head to inside if possible for kick-out block. If defensive end closes, log blocks, working his hips outside.

Power vs. Odd Front

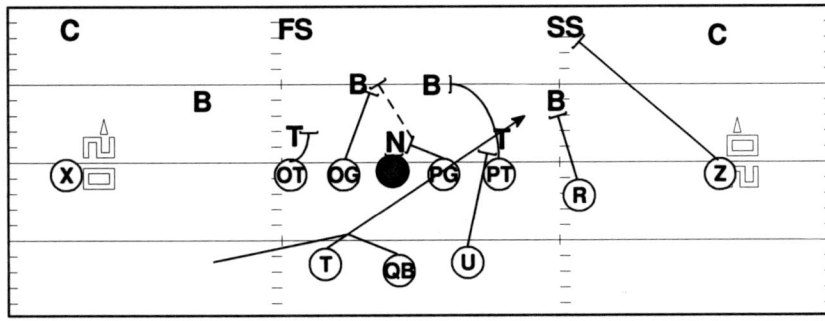

Figure 19-8

Assignments:

PT: Recognizes depth of inside linebacker. Must get head to playside of inside linebacker. Anticipates flow of inside linebacker.

PG: Double-teams with center. Ensures double-team, then comes off on backside inside linebacker. Exactly like trap block.

C: Double-teams with playside guard. Ensures double-team. Comes off to backside inside linebacker if noseguard slants strong.

OG: Great angle to backside inside linebacker. Gets head to playside.

OT: Reach blocks on defensive tackle. If unable to reach, then gets a tie down the line of scrimmage.

U: Takes inside path to defensive end. Gets head to inside hip. If defensive end closes, log blocks, getting hips around.

Sweep vs. Even Front

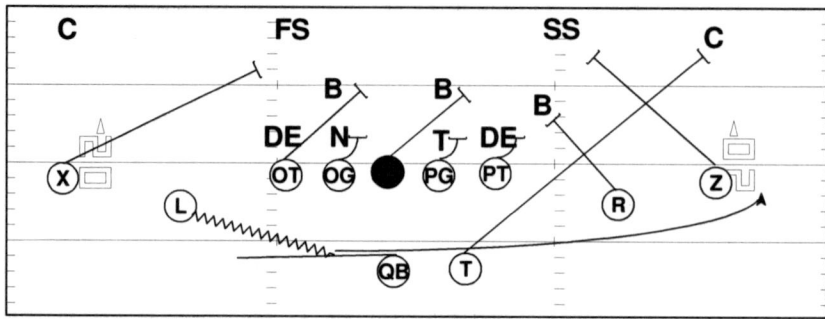

Figure 19-9

Assignments:

PT: Flat reach blocks. Pulls and overtakes defensive end. Gets head to playside.

PG: Flat reach blocks. Pulls and overtakes defensive tackle. Gets head to playside.

C: Sharp angle to cut off playside inside linebacker.

OG: Flat reach blocks. Pulls and overtakes noseguard. Gets head to playside.

OT: Sharp angle to cut off backside inside linebacker. Disregards defensive end. Tries to cross backside inside linebacker face.

Sweep vs. Odd Front

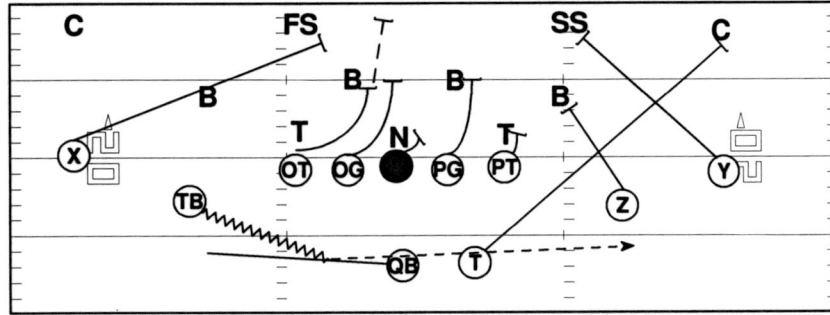

Figure 19-10

Assignments:

PT: Reach blocks on defensive tackle. Works head to outside. If unable to get head outside, gets a tie and works down the line of scrimmage. Possible arc block.

PG: Anticipates depth and angle of inside linebacker. Adjusts angle to get head to playside of inside linebacker. Cuts him off at the pass, and stick on him. Doesn't dive. Runs with him while blocking. Must be a pest!

C: Reach blocks on noseguard. Works head to playside. If unable to get head playside, then gets a tie and works down the line of scrimmage.

OG: Anticipates depth and angle of inside linebacker. Adjusts angle to get head to playside of inside linebacker. Cuts him off at the pass, and sticks on him. Doesn't dive. Runs with him while blocking. Must be a pest!

OT: Disregards defensive tackle and tries to get to inside linebacker. If offensive guard gets to inside linebacker, then works up to free safety.

APPENDIX

Motivational Quotes

"When you see a successful individual, a champion, you can be very sure that you are looking at an individual who pays great attention to the perfection of minor details."

—John Wooden

"Every day of hard work is like putting money in the bank; you want to have money in the bank when you go to cash the check."

—Bill Belichik

"Showing up is 90 percent of the deal."

—Rich Frank

"Man's greatest moment of happiness is to be tested beyond what he thought might be his breaking point and not fail."

—Joseph Murphy

"Sometimes less is more. It's true in cooking, and it's true in life."

—Hans Schmidt

"For the play to work, you must work the play."

—Patty "Cakes" Johnston

"The strength of the group is the strength of the leaders."

—Vince Lombardi

"Loudly praise, softly criticize."

—Ming Demoe

"Motivating through fear may work in the short term to get people to do something, but over the long run I believe personal pride is a much greater motivator. It produces far better results that last for a much longer time."

—John Wooden

"Practice under some coaches runs for three hours. Mine lasted an hour and a half to two hours, and we always finished on time. If practice does not end when it is supposed to end, players will hold back a little effort and energy. I wanted my players to give their best effort throughout practice, so I became a stickler for time management. As a result my players knew how long practice would run and worked harder during the scheduled time. By having practices carefully orchestrated and always ending on time, we got more done in a shorter period of time. If we are going to become all that we are capable of becoming, we need to work hard, but we also need to be intentional about the hard work. Planning places effort where effort is most needed."

—John Wooden

"Don't tell me how rough the water is; just bring the ship in."

—Chuck Knox

"Your first job as a new coach should be to create a culture of success. You must model, communicate, teach, reward, and enforce the expectations and standards for how your program will operate, including how your athletes will train, practice, compete, win, lose, lead, and conduct themselves on and off the playing field."

—Bill Walsh

"Do not confuse activity with achievement."

—John Wooden

"The quality of a person's life is in direct proportion to his commitment to excellence, regardless of his chosen field of endeavor."

—Vince Lombardi

"It's not who you know or what you know; it's that you never know."

—Jaime Minuusch

"The time will come when winter will ask what you were doing all summer."

—Henry Clay, American statesman

"Diversity is the spice of life."

—Herc Hanifin

"Coach each boy as if he were your own son."

—Eddie Robinson

"The speed of the leader determines the rate of the pack."

—Unknown

"Good coaching is based purely in leadership … a positive example … and instilling respect in your players."

—John Wooden

"Don't tell me about the pain; just bring the baby home."

—Hondo Barflux

"My responsibility is leadership, and the minute I get negative, that is going to have an influence on my team."

—Don Shula

"You can motivate players better with kind words than you can with a whip."

—Bud Wilkinson

"Players don't care how much I know until they know how much I care."

—Frosty Westering

"It's not what the coach knows that counts, but rather what the players have learned."

—Amos Alonzo Stagg

*"No written word
Nor spoken plea
Can teach our youths
What they should be.*

*Nor all the books
On all the shelves.
It's what the teachers
Are themselves"*

—Unknown

"A real friend is one who helps us think our best thoughts, do our noblest deeds, and be our finest selves."

—Unknown

"Commitment to the team: there is no such thing as in-between; you are either in or out."

—Pat Riley

"The coach's most powerful tool is love."

—John Wooden

"No coach who is sure of himself and his team constantly bawls out his players."

—Jock Sutherland

"Winners do the things that losers don't want or like to do. Winners perform tasks that losers don't even if they are difficult and unpleasant. They do them because they are necessary for victory."

—Craig Johnston

"I've come to a frightening conclusion that I am the decisive element in the classroom. It's my personal approach that creates the climate. It's my daily mood that makes the weather. As a teacher, I possess a tremendous power to make a child's life miserable or joyous. I can be a tool of torture or an instrument of inspiration. I can humiliate or humor, hurt or heal. In all situations, it is my response that decides whether a crisis will be escalated or deescalated and a child humanized or dehumanized."

—Haim Ginott

"Love your players, or get out of coaching."

—Bobby Dodd

"Leadership must be demonstrated, not announced."

—Fran Tarkenton

"You become your choices. Your choices become habits. Make good choices, and you develop good habits."

—Shambe Wright-Faire

"When you find your opponent's weak spot, hammer it."

—John Heisman

"Be what he isn't."

—Hans Schmidt

"The greatest of all faults is to be conscious of none."

—Thomas Carlyle, English author

"You can't make a great play unless you do it first in practice."

—Chuck Noll

"If you know the enemy and know yourself, you need not fear the result of a hundred battles."

—Sun Tzu

"Practice without improvement is meaningless."

—Chuck Knox

"Put your information across slowly, and repeat it over and over again! Take a difficult point and make it so simple that it will become clear to even the dullard."

—Knute Rockne

"In battle there are not more than two methods of attack—the direct and the indirect, yet these two in combination give rise to an endless series of maneuvers."

—Sun Tzu

"A team should never practice on a field that is not lined. Your players have to become aware of the field's boundaries."

—John Madden

"Fighting with a large army is no different than fighting with a small one: it is merely a question of instituting signs and signals."

—Sun Tzu

"Beat 'em to the punch."

—Bill Walsh

"The true test of character is not how much we know how to do, but how we behave when we don't know what to do."

—John Holt

"Industriousness is the most conscientious, assiduous, and inspired type of work. A willingness to, an appetite for, hard work must be present for success. Without it, you have nothing to build on."

—John Wooden

"The quarterback is like an artist. The artist controls what goes where on the canvas. The quarterback controls what goes where on the gridiron. His focus is on his receivers downfield, and the on-rushers become a swirl of colors beneath the main vision."

—Steve Clarkson

"Our mistakes don't make or break us. If we are lucky, they simply reveal who we really are, what we're really made of."

—Donn Moomaw

"ENTHUSIASM is the fire in our furnace, it is the spark that keeps us going in high gear. It makes going great.
Enthusiasm brings on Excitement
Excitement then produces Energy
Energy generates Extra Effort
Extra effort develops Excellence"

—Frosty Westering

"If you want to see a fighter at his best, watch him when he is getting beat."
—Sugar Ray Robinson

"Timing has a lot to do with the outcome of a rain dance."

—Unknown

"Regard your soldiers as children, and they may follow you wherever you may lead. Look upon them as beloved sons and they will stand by you unto death."

—Sun Tzu

"You can't stop at every dog that barks, or you'll never get the mail delivered."
—Phog Allen

About the Author

Craig Johnston was an all-state quarterback at St. Paul High School in Santa Fe Springs, California in 1976 where he accumulated a 51-3 record over four years. His nationally ranked team had a 13-1 record, playing the Division 4A CIF championship game in the Los Angeles Coliseum. That summer, Johnston played in the North-South Shrine All-Star football game in the Pasadena Rose Bowl, where he led his team to victory.

Johnston went on to be a three-year starter at quarterback and three-year captain at Cal Poly San Luis Obispo, leading his team to a Division II national championship in 1980. (This is still Cal Poly's only football national championship in its 93 years of competition.) He finished his career at Cal Poly as the all-time leader in passing and total offense. He was inducted into the Cal Poly Athletics Hall of Fame in 2015.

Johnston's coaching career started early when, in 1979, he became a "player" quarterback coach at Cal Poly while redshirting and recovering from knee surgery between his junior and senior year of eligibility.

From 1981 to 1983, Johnston joined his college head coach Joe Harper and high school head coach Marijon Ancich at Northern Arizona University, where he coached quarterback Scott Lindquist, who was signed by the Los Angeles Raiders, and wide receiver Pete Mandley, the nations Division IAA total offense leader, drafted by the Detroit Lions.

From NAU, Johnston returned to Cal Poly San Luis Obispo to coach quarterbacks with head coach Jim Sanderson from 1983 to 1984. He coached quarterback Tim Snodgrass, who broke his single-season passing record.

In 1998, Johnston was offensive coordinator at Monterey Peninsula College in Monterey, California. His SNH attack was the key to an instant turnaround, which resulted in a conference championship and bowl game appearance.

Johnston was the head football coach at Carmel High School in Carmel, California for 18 years, acquiring numerous county and league Coach of the Year honors while sending many players to the college ranks. Johnston's no-huddle system was the first of its kind in a highly competitive football area and has stood the test of time. In the last five years, Carmel has been one of the highest scoring teams in the state of California, averaging over 50 points per game and 5,000 yards of offense per year

Johnston's sons Pat, Phil, and Ken accounted for more than 15,000 yards of high school SNH offense. Quarterbacks Ken and Pat combining for 144 passing touchdowns and 13,000 yards, while wide receiver Phil accounted for over 2,000 yards and 140 receptions. All three played football for Cal Poly San Luis Obispo.

Johnston has been married to his wife Patty "Cakes" for 30 years.